101

REAL

ESTATE

TIPS

SAM HACHEM

REALTOR

MAXWELL

PROGRESSIVE

REALTY

DEDICATIONS

TO ALL OF MY FRIENDS AND FAMILY. THANK YOU FOR YOUR CONTINUED SUPPORTS AND REFERRALS.

COPYRIGHT 2021

CONTENTS

THE END

INTRODUCTION

'Welcome to the book that will educate you'

In the ever-changing world of real estate, it's important to always remember that the smallest decisions can sometimes make the biggest difference. Educating yourself on the business of real estate can save you much unneeded stress, and at the same time provide you with financial freedom while living your best life, as a homeowner.

As you venture into the world of real estate, you will find this writing handy as you navigate through all the potential trappings this world can provide. If you are a seasoned pro, you will find these tips useful and entertaining. You may have lived through experiences like the ones highlighted within the walls of these words. Either way, your experience in real estate should be a positive one.

In the combined 2 decades of experience that I have as licensed Realtor, I have come up with '101 Real Estate Tips.' These are straight-forward situations and circumstances that you will surely encounter on your way to owning your home and/or building your portfolio.

In real estate, it can be exceedingly difficult to predict when issues arise, and you need to get ahead of any potential problems before they become problems. For this reason, we go to all situations with the tips provided. There will be no flow in the writing, and it's purposely designed that way.

In the real world of real estate, you can try as much as you can to keep the flow, but there will always be issues that arise and command your attention. Especially since your transaction may include an emotional side. This could be draining to you emotionally, mentally, and physically, because you are having to deal with issues that could have been dealt with earlier in the process.

I am here to help you. I hope you enjoy reading these words and feel free to always call or email me with any questions.

TIP #1

'Where and how do I start my journey?'

This could be the most crucial tip of them all. Where do you start? It's no secret that in modern society, almost everyone starts their real estate search online. You may have recently visited your friend that that has just purchased a home, and upon further thought, you have decided to take the plunge and buy a home yourself.

There is nothing wrong with going online and searching out information within your initial stages of interest. Just beware of all the misleading advertising and gimmicks that you may come across. For example, some real estate companies want you to sign an online agreement to receive specified information. DO NOT GET HOOKED INTO THIS!

If you are in your initial stages of learning about real estate, do not sign anything with anyone! The fact is, there are many sources from which you can retrieve valuable information. Most notably, you can learn from a great Realtor or mortgage broker.

The first thing you can do is ask the people that you know regarding their experiences. They will give you their honest opinion about their purchase and provide you with their own view on their experience with the professionals they dealt with. This includes the Realtor, mortgage broker, home inspector, lawyer, and insurance agent.

If your peers have had a good experience with any of the above, do not hesitate to get in touch with any or all of them at the beginning of your process. If they gave your peers great service, chances are, they will do the same for you. They will also be looking out for your best interests a lot more than someone you just 'googled.'

<u>TIP #2</u>

'Have the right attitude and be positive'

The home buying process should not be a stressful experience at all. It makes absolutely no sense to go into it without a positive attitude. Furthermore, it should be a fun and joyful experience. Especially if you are a first-time home buyer. Remember, this is an experience that you want to share with your children, the story of how you acquired the home they grew up in. So, make it memorable in the right way.

All too often, we hear stories from people who had a negative experience investing in real estate. There could be several reasons why. First and foremost, hiring the right professionals is key. If you were to hire a REALTOR that was impatient, for example, then your experience will not be a fun one at all.

Imagine going into a car dealership to look at cars, and having the salesperson breathe down your neck pushing you to write an offer. Imagine walking into a clothing store to look at shirts and having the customer care associate breathe down your neck pushing you to make a purchase. Imagine going into a restaurant and having the server be rude, pushing you to order something fast, so that they can go check on the other tables and make larger tips.

Don't hesitate in firing someone that you are not comfortable with. Seriously, I will say it again, DON'T HESITATE IN FIRING SOMEONE YOU ARE NOT COMFORTABLE WITH! You will be exposed to different professionals along your path to home ownership. Having great people along the way will make the process that much more enjoyable and comfortable.

TIP #3

'Real estate TV can be unrealistic'

As professionals in the real estate industry, we get asked all the time about our thoughts regarding TV shows centered around real estate. To be honest, they really glorify the state of how transactions work. There are all sorts of shows out there too, shows centered on first-time home buyers, as well as shows centered around flipping homes.

This is all great TV, so don't avoid it. It's just that different shows are filmed in different markets. Things tend to work differently wherever you go. For example, a show about flipping houses may show you the following:

Purchase price	$250,000
Renovation cost	$35,000
Final sale price	$340,000
Total profit	$55,000

For sake of this point, an amazingly simple example has been provided. This is the basis of what these

TV shows teach you. Along the process, they show you some of the pitfalls and such that you may come across, such as finding problems they weren't expecting. Problems such as mold in the bathrooms or mice in the basement, things of that nature.

But what they don't show you is the financial stress that you may encounter. When using the bank's money, you need to make payments that include interest. You need to pay utility costs and taxes. Upon selling, you have real estate and lawyer fees. Some jurisdictions even have land transfer tax. Have you ever heard of land transfer tax? Point made.

We can't always believe what we see on TV. Sure, it can be very educational, but learning your own marketplace is essential before having dreams of world domination in real estate. Learn your market!

TIP #4

'Emotions should help, not hinder'

Making the dive into real estate can be a very emotional experience. They say you should never make a business decision based on emotions, but in real estate, it happens all the time. Especially for first-time home buyers.

When you have a husband and wife looking for a home that they intend to raise their family in, it's a good bet that emotions could potentially run high. That's Ok, there is nothing wrong with that. It is completely normal to get emotional when you are looking for the home your family will be raised in. Just don't let your emotions take over completely.

If you are qualified to buy a $400,000 home, those are the parameters you need to stay within. If your friends bought a $500,000 home, good for them. If a $500,000 home is not in the cards for you, then so be it. Everyone's circumstances are different. If you want a $500,000 home, but only can afford a

$400,000 home, then maybe the time is not right for you to buy.

Managing expectations during an emotional business time like this can be difficult. We will get more into that in the next chapter. Sometimes, you may find yourself in a situation where you are competing for a home, multiple offers. If not handled correctly, it can be very heart-wrenching.

Sometimes, things are meant to be, and sometimes they are not. It is not the end of the world if you go into multiple offers on a home and not win. Nobody wants to overpay anyway, so why should you? There are times, however, when a home comes up that is too good to pass up. When this happens, there is no shame in putting your best foot forward, just confirm value before submitting your offer. I can always help with this, don't hesitate to ask me.

Your emotions should help you choose your house. Upon walking in, that feeling you get when you fall in love is a special feeling. This is the emotion you want to use when purchasing. Don't get upset over the home you can't afford, be happy with the home that is meant for you.

TIP #5

'Manage your expectations wisely'

Expectations must always be managed wisely and in such a way that you don't end up disappointed in the end. Humans tend to push the envelope and 'max out' on their purchases. This is true with clothing, cars, and of course, homes. In fact, over 90% of home buyers make their purchase at the maximum amount in which they are qualified for.

The problems arise when the expectations exceed your budget. Therefore, it is imperative to call me, your local expert, to gain an understanding of the marketplace and distinguish between what is affordable and what isn't. The managing of expectations goes further than this.

When going through the transaction, your expectations for different scenarios throughout the process must be contained. At any point in the transaction, your resolve and patience will be tested. For example, if you have found a house and made an offer, financing approved, the inspection comes last. What happens if the inspection doesn't go the way you had hoped?

Home inspections can be extremely dramatic. As a buyer, you need to understand that it doesn't matter how new or old the home is, there is potential for problems. In 2004, we represented a buyer that was purchasing a 2002 built home. Upon inspection, we found a moisture problem in one of the bathrooms. The buyer was shocked. Thankfully, we were able to solve that situation. Believe it or not, the buyer didn't want to do the inspection originally until I was able to convince him to do so.

Always expect the unexpected. When you are surrounded by the right professionals, you will be more prepared to handle situations that arise. If you never over-expect, then you'll never be disappointed.

TIP #6

'Become a student of the game'

Educating yourself on the business of real estate is highly recommended. After all, in the end, it is YOU that needs to make the final decision on purchasing your home. It is YOU that needs to come up with the down payment. It is YOU that needs to hire the Realtor, mortgage broker, home inspector, and lawyer. Everything is on you to call the final shot.

It's ok to ask questions. Ask as many questions as you like! Part of the job of your hired professionals is to use their expertise to answer your questions throughout the process. They will be able to give you all the knowledge you need to complete the process of buying. I will do this!

Don't be afraid to ask 'strange' questions. When you are trying to get your head around some of the steps toward your purchase, then you will want to feel comfortable at every step. The only way to do this is to have your questions answered.

Reading is another way you can add to your knowledge of real estate. There aren't many books out there that will cater to your specific market, so always confirm things with me before you accept the material you read. I can also provide you with a copy of my first real estate book, *'Real Estate Simplified.'* I originally wrote this in 2009 and many principles are still consistent with how things are done today. It is a timeless writing.

This current book of tips is perfectly designed to help you in your marketplace. You can use the tools you learn in this book when you are purchasing anywhere in Western Canada. Whether you are in Edmonton, Alberta, or Vancouver, B.C. The basic tips you will learn in this book are timeless as well. The best part is that you can always ask me to expand on the tips you read here.

TIP #7

'Assuming never helps, always confirm'

Sometimes, the smallest details can become the biggest headaches if they are not confirmed properly. When it comes to even the smallest of details, confirm! Confirm! Confirm! Confirm! There are so many general circumstances where bits of information slip through the cracks and you find out later that the information you were given was invalid.

If you were buying a house that had a finished basement, you would want to know if the basement has permits. In the moment of looking at the house, the general emotion and excitement might overcome you to the point where you forget to ask this question before emotionally committing to the home. This could be problematic.

As a licensed REALTOR for 2 decades, I would make sure to confirm the status of the basement permits and explain the outcomes of why it is so important to know these things. Moving forward if you were looking at taking your basement to the next level to make a basement suite. Not having permits already in place could cost you big money.

If your basement is finished but the electrical has been done wrong, then you may be forced to tear out the walls and redo the electrical from top to bottom. If your house burns down and it is found to be the result of faulty wiring, then your insurance company may give you a hard time when it comes to them paying out.

Missing a detail such as permits is a common issue when it comes to people buying homes for the first time. You get wrapped up in all the excitement and before you know it, you are in love with a house that has no proper permits in the basement. Please remember that every minor detail counts. Don't assume everything will be fine, confirm it! I will point these things out during showings, so I'll be your safety net.

TIP #8

'Privacy rules are in place for your safety'

Typically, buyers always seem to ask why a seller is selling their home. This is private information and most real estate jurisdictions around the world have privacy laws in effect to protect the privacy of consumers. So, when you ask why someone is selling, they are not hiding anything by not telling you. They are simply protecting their privacy. They are more than welcome to share their reasons by their own free will and accord. But that's it.

This is different than if they were hiding the fact that there is mold in the house, or a mice problem, or anything of that nature doing with the structure and safety of the home. Hiding personal information is quite different from hiding information on a home you are about to sell for a lot of money.

Everyone that works for you is obligated to protect your privacy! This becomes quite evident when dealing on real estate that involves divorces, estate sales, probate sales, etc.... Anything that involves family can sometimes get quite sticky.

Let's use 'estate sales' for example. An 'estate sale' is the liquidation of a home that belonged to a person who has died. Their 'next of kin' is entitled to the property and thus the process of selling the property and splitting all the dividends fairly is important. Sometimes, families get into huge fights over property and assets left behind.

As your trusted professional, I understand the importance of your privacy and will maintain that privacy over and above any circumstance that tries pushing us to give up the information. We will always understand the meaning of privacy.

TIP #9

'Values can change at any time'

If you were to get a Comparative Market Analysis (CMA) on your home, don't count on that value staying current past 6 months. The fact is markets change and fluctuate at any time. It is exceedingly difficult to predict what the market will do, beyond knowing that spring times are busy.

Today, your home might be worth $425,000 based on the knowledge that 2 remarkably similar homes recently sold in your neighborhood. The homes sold for $422,000 and $429,000, respectively. There are other factors involved when determining price, but we will use these numbers for the sake of making this point.

Fast forward 6 months, and another similar home sells for $395,000. Does this change the value of your home? The answer is simple. Yes, it does change the value of your home. Chances are the buyer that is looking to buy your home looks at comparable sales within 6 months of them preparing an offer.

The buyer will see the first 2 homes that sold, and they will see the last one. Do you think they will try to use that last sale to help negotiate your house down? You bet they will! They certainly will not want to pay $425,000 for it. Don't worry, however, because this works the other way too. If the latest home sale went for $450,000, then as the seller, you have reason to fight for that higher price.

Values constantly change, and it will always be that way. The market will always adjust to seasons. If you are wondering about other circumstances such as 'COVID-19,' yes pandemics do adjust the market as well. 'COVID-19' didn't affect the market as much as people would think. Unless the world comes to an end, then your home will always have value. We will get more into this later in the book.

TIP #10

'Avoid getting ripped off by shady people'

Like it or not, there are always going to be shady people in the world of Real Estate. Early in my career, I had a young couple who shared a very disappointing story of theirs. About 2 years before I met them, they had decided to try and purchase a home privately. This was direct from a seller who told them that they would 'save' on the commissions by buying privately.

They had met this guy through a friend at their work. They arranged to see the house, and after that, they gave him a $2000 deposit. Keep in mind, this was a young couple starting out and earning low incomes. $2000 was a lot of money to them. As they went through the buying process, their bank had some concerns over the value of the home.

They were purchasing the home at a price of $270,000, yet the bank had shown a value of not more than $230,000. The young couple were shocked. So, they called the seller and asked for their deposit back, but he refused. In the contract that they had signed, it was stipulated that the deposit was 'non-refundable.' They didn't know this and didn't realize at the time of signing, that they'd never see that money again. They took their case to small claims court and lost. At the same time, they took both an emotional hit and a financial hit through this situation.

The seller in this case was a real piece of scum. I personally hate when guys like him try to take advantage of people that aren't educated in the ways of real estate. I can spot these guys a mile away. Their lies and dishonesty eventually catch up to them.

TIP #11

'Be humble in times of growth and glory'

Greed can eventually lead to downfall. It has happened in many such cases in life and in business. If you are selling in a hot market, be careful, avoid the 'greed factor.' Anytime the market gets hot, you might find yourself reviewing multiple offers on your home. But it might just be an illusion, I'll explain.

If the market hits a point where you are seeing 5 offers on every house that comes up, keep in mind that 3 of these offers may not be an offer by legitimate buyers. Quite possibly, they could be offers by people who are jumping on the bandwagon of the hot market. They read online that it's a good time to buy. These buyers are people that wouldn't buy in a regular market.

The problem starts when these guys must put their money down. On Sunday night, they got caught up in all the hype and emotion. They made a whopping offer of $15,000 above list price! They beat all the other offers and you chose them. Great? Hold on a second.

The next day, they wake up and they start to doubt their decision. Maybe they paid too much? Their Realtor calls them to pick up the deposit cheque, and they get no answer. Silence. What happens now? At this point, the house goes back on the market.

Of the original 5 offers, the winning bid is now gone. On top of that, 2 of the remaining 4 offers have decided not to come back. They are upset at the events of the night before, they are out. Remember how I said these things can get emotional? This leaves 2 offers now. Will you get $15,000 above list? Unlikely. In fact, you may not get above list price today. Last night, you might have had you chosen the right offer.

TIP #12

'Don't base your decision off the pictures'

This happens all the time, a new listing comes up hot and fresh on the market! The pictures look fantastic, and you are ready to make an offer even before you view the house! It's totally Ok to be this excited. But, at the same time, please contain your emotions until you view the property!

If you want so much to like it, then you might look past the faults that might be clear and in plain view. For example, you might really like a particular property, but you are told that a jail might be built across the street. I know this might be an extreme example, but it highlights the point.

In your excitement, you might look past this issue and brush it off. Or you might ask me if it's even 100% true, with the hope that I tell you that the plans for a jail are not yet approved. Even that little glimmer of hope might be all you need to help make your final decision.

It's important to walk into each property with a fresh set of eyes. I'm not saying to completely discount what you saw in the pictures. I'm just saying that you should take the time to validate your findings. Is that too much to ask? Is that room really that big? Is that yard really that big? Believe me when I say this, wide-angle cameras can work wonders.

A picture can tell you a thousand words, but it may not always speak the truth. The pictures are used to get you through the door, so viewing the pictures online is vital in helping narrow down your search. If photos aren't clear, it doesn't mean they are trying to hide anything, it just means they used a poor-quality camera. As technology increases, this issue will be less as we move forward into the future.

TIP #13

'Advertisements for lists of foreclosures'

People advertising 'exclusive' foreclosure lists are misleading you. Investors do this to attract 'rent-to-own' prospects and Realtors do this to attract buyer clients. The truth is, ALL FORECLOSURE LISTINGS GO THROUGH ORGANIZED REAL ESTATE! This list is something I can provide you, just ask me.

In our world of keeping things fair, all foreclosures get listed on REALTOR.CA in Canada and REALTOR.COM in the United States. The reason is simple, banks don't want people using inside information to try and 'score' the property for a low price, without letting the home go to market and everyone have a fair shot at offering on it.

There is no special information that any Realtor or mortgage broker can provide to you that is exclusive to them. We all have access to the same information. I am more than happy to give you all the information you require and answer any of your questions.

Personally, I hate misleading advertising. It's a very dishonest and ruthless way of doing business. Even worse, the only people that lose in these scenarios are the consumers, you. It's disappointing when you see an advertisement that explains things a certain way, and you come to find out that it's not entirely true.

It's like if you were to read an advertisement from a car dealership that stated they are selling brand new cars for $5000. Would you call them? I would. By the time you call them, they give you some stupid excuse about how the advertisement is structured and it means something completely different. But they now have you on the phone as a 'buyer prospect.' Maybe they can sell you something else.

I don't trust misleading advertising and I never will. I'm not even comfortable doing business with people that put such ads out there, and nor should you.

TIP #14

'Negotiating tactics that are false'

"Hey! There's another offer coming so you need to decide right now!" Have you ever heard this before? If so, it's vitally important to get confirmation of that other offer prior to proceeding. In 2007, the Canadian Real Estate Association came under heavy scrutiny due to people in the industry claiming to have other 'phantom offers.'

These days, it must be disclosed if there are any truthful offers. If you ever come across a salesperson who is pushing you by saying there are other people that are wanting to buy the same house, then fine, tell them to keep it. You are not going to be pushed!

Like it or not, we see these tactics all the time, in both residential and commercial real estate. However, I must say that there are times when there is truly another offer or interested party at the table. But just leave that to me to confirm, it's my job.

When the market is busy, there's a good probability chance that there is high interest in a property that you are deciding on. At the same time, we will pull out comparable homes that have sold in the area to help us determine value. By determining value, it will be easy for us to see if the property in question does indeed have a lot of interest. Price tells the story.

I have run into situations where I have suspected 'phantom offers.' I always make sure that everything is documented and disclosed. It's important that the customer is always 100% aware of exactly what's going on during negotiations. I will say it again, you will not be pushed!

TIP #15

'Home inspection surprises are common'

I always tell people that home inspections can get 'dramatic.' It doesn't matter whether the house is 5 years old or 50 years old, issues might arise. Homes are built to withstand a lot of wear and tear, but still, age gets to them. It's important for any buyer, or seller, in the marketplace to understand that issues may arise in the inspection.

Let's start with homeowners. I have witnessed utter shock in their reactions when learning of issues that have come up in the home that they are selling. Most sellers aren't out trying to hide anything, they simply aren't aware of deficiencies sometimes. For example, if a home inspector finds that the insulation in the attic is too low, the homeowner might be surprised because, in the 10 years they lived in the house, they never had an issue.

I always do my best to coach my sellers to be prepared for a scenario like this. They could possibly have the perfect house, but a good inspector will always find something. You can't get mad at them, it's their job. If a customer is paying them $500 to inspect the house, then I'm sure the inspector will do their best to make sure the customer gets the best inspection possible. Full disclosure is especially important.

For buyers, it is key to understand that no house is perfect. There will be issues that arise that are not visible to the naked eye. There is no point to go and renegotiate after the inspection shows some burnt out light bulbs and loose taps in the bathroom. Obviously, if there are major issues, then you would need to have them addressed. A good example of a major issue would be the electrical system. If it isn't up to code, then it's important to get an electrician in to bring it up to code.

TIP #16

'The myth of buying at low interest rates'

Have you ever been told how important it is to buy before interest rates go up? Sure, it's important to lock in a good interest rate but be aware regarding the state of the market at the point of which you are buying. Beyond rates, the market itself fluctuates constantly.

When rates are low, everyone is buying. Think about this, what does that do to home values? Yes, home values rise when interest rates are low. Does this mean you are still making a sound purchase? First, it's important to know and understand the state of the market which you are buying in. Is it busy or is it slow? This is a question I can easily answer for you 7 days per week, 365 days per year.

I will fast forward. I would rather buy at a lower price, when interest rates are higher, as compared to buying at a higher price, with a lower interest rate. If I'm looking at a 1.9% interest rate at time of purchase, I want to buy. But would I buy at a 3%

interest rate for the same purchase price? No. What if my purchase price was $50,000 less?

In real estate, there are no missed opportunities if you position yourself properly in the market. Understanding interest rates is not just about straight numbers. You need to understand where the market is going and where your opportunities are so you can buy at the lowest possible price.

If you open your news application on your smart phone and read that the market is slow, then it's a great time to buy! Who cares about the interest rate, it's not going to increase by any crazy amount! The price you purchase at could be dropped significantly should you choose to buy at the right time.

TIP #17

'The right time of the week to view properties'

The times you go to view properties doesn't really affect the process unless it's a weekend during the busy spring season. Back in the early days of real estate, people would spend their evenings and weekends looking at homes. Even up to the 1980s and 1990s, evenings and weekends were the norm over 80% of the time. But times have changed.

In the modern era (post-2000) showings happen at all different times. The reason for this is simple, the work landscape has changed. Gone are the days of 9-5 workdays for mass population. There are now more people working shiftwork, seasonal jobs, and working from home. For these reasons, flexibility in showing times has varied.

A good example would be banks. They used to be open Monday to Friday 9am-5pm. In the modern era, there are some banks that are open 7 days per week! This is evident even in the post-COVID-19 world as well. With the increased hours, banks need to spread out their working hours over a 7-day period, not 5 days.

To be fair, a bank worker might be scheduled to work 3 weekdays, 1 weeknight, and 1 weekend day per week. A schedule like this would leave that bank worker available to view homes at some point during the week, as they are only tied up for 3 weekdays.

In my career, I have done showings as early as 6am and as late as 10pm. While its not always ideal to view properties when it is dark outside, sometimes a clients' schedule pushes us in the direction of early and late-night showings. This is especially true during the busy springtime. Sometimes, you can't wait until the weekend to view a property, because it may go pending before.

There is no right or wrong time to view properties. But remember that it is always important to be on the ball and go see a property sooner rather than later. It's disappointing when you miss out on a property due to a delayed showing request time.

TIP #18

'Estate sales and probate sales'

When a homeowner passes away, if their affairs are not taken care of before their time of passing, then the home will likely go into 'probate' or an 'estate' sale. They are both essentially the same thing, going through a lawyer to legally sell the home on behalf of the estate of the person who passed.

Generally, these homes can be fantastic deals in terms of pricing. In fact, the price you can get on a 'probate' or 'estate' sale can rival the pricing you can get on a foreclosure. Sometimes, 'probate' sales and 'estate' sales could be the best deals you can get in real estate. In my time as a Realtor, I have seen some super cheap 'probate' and 'estate' sales come to market. Some of them I have seen sell for over $100,000 less than the tax assessed value!

Why are these homes so cheap? It's simple, you are buying from a person or people that have inherited this asset. They never had to work for this property, pay the mortgage and taxes. They never had to do the general upkeep. They inherited this asset and now it's time to cash out! It could be one 'next-of-kin,' or there could be more people involved. Any way you look at it, they want their money!

When its time to sell, they ask the lawyer simply "How fast do we get our money?" Now this isn't true in all cases. Families are dealing with the grief of losing their loved one, so this could potentially be an emotionally charged endeavor for them. But in the end, they just want to move on. And what better way to move on then to drop the price to sell quick.

As a buyer this is how you can benefit. Putting yourself in a position to buy a property like that at a steep discount. In real estate, we hear the word 'foreclosure' as being the ultimate word. In many cases, it is the ultimate word in real estate. At the same time, don't forget these other words that could be beneficial to you.

TIP #19

'The drawbacks of hiring a cheap lawyer'

Different lawyers come with different costs. Their normal fee can vary, while the disbursement costs are consistent. If a lawyer has good rates and is good at what they do, then there's no reason not to use them. If a lawyer is a bit more expensive but they come highly recommended, don't be cheap. Seriously, you get what you pay for.

There are a lot of fantastic lawyers in our marketplace. Be sure to use one that specializes in real estate law. They know all the ins and outs of the real estate transaction and they won't miss any details. They use a systematic approach and make sure that everything happens on schedule.

Early in my career, one of my clients used a 'part-time' lawyer that was super cheap. I warned them against this and to check around with other lawyers, just to give themselves some options. They decided that the price was too good to pass up, and they stuck with the cheap guy. Did they live to regret it? Yes, they did.

When closing day came, their lawyer was nowhere to be found. In fact, the lawyer took the day off! I am not kidding here; this is a true story. The clients were supposed to take possession on that day, which was a Friday, so they ended up having to wait until Monday to get the keys.

To make matters worse, they had to stay in a hotel over the weekend and had their things locked up in a truck outside the hotel for 3 straight nights! What a headache. All this because they wanted to save some money in lawyer costs. Not worth it.

I'm telling you right now, don't hesitate to pay a lawyer their worth! Don't settle for second rate. Now, just to be clear, this was the only time in my career that I encountered an issue of this magnitude with a lawyer not being around. I have been exposed to many great lawyers in my career. Trust that your marketplace has many fantastic lawyers, so you have plenty to choose from.

TIP #20

'Be sure to ask plenty of questions'

This relates to what we discussed earlier regarding becoming a student of the game. There are no stupid questions. In fact, I want you to ask me as many questions as possible. I would relish the fact that you ask me questions. It's better for you anyways, because it will help give you a better understanding of the process moving forward.

Also, feel free to ask me the same question multiple times. Seriously, I don't mind. Whatever it takes to get you to understand the process better, we will do. This is more important for first-time home buyers. You have never been through the process, so it is essential to collect as much information as possible.

I'll go as far as saying that if you encounter anyone along your way that is impatient, fire them. In the real estate transaction, you will be exposed to several professionals. Realtor (me), lawyer, mortgage broker, home inspector, insurance broker, etc. Be sure to choose your professionals wisely.

All your professionals should be ready and prepared to answer all your questions. That is their job, to answer your questions. I have met many great professionals in my years as a Realtor. I find that the more experienced ones are better equipped to answer your questions in a fashion that will be easy to understand.

Ask away when it comes to the questions you have on your mind. Whether it's through talk, text, or email, send your questions through. Even late at night, if you have a question on your mind that is bothering you until you get it answered, then get a hold of me. I'm here to help.

TIP #21

'Is the price of land always going up?'

The market is always changing. Prices fluctuate all the time. In some years, you will find the prices to be high and multiple offers are the norm. In other years, you'll find there to be plenty of homes on the market and they are listed at decent prices. The market never stays the same and it can be exceedingly difficult to predict.

The value of land does go up over time. When you factor in inflation, interest rates, and economic changes such as what consumers want. In the early 2000s, condos were all the rage. It appeared everyone wanted a condo. Low maintenance, easy to rent, and not much overhead.

Fast forward 2 decades later, and condos are still showing value, but builders have adjusted what they build. These days, there are a lot more residential attached properties that don't have condo fees. Condo fees are the killer. A condo building with high condo fees make it difficult to sell at high prices in the future. A $300 condo fee is manageable, a $500 condo fee is expensive.

Overall, if you look back at values over the years, you will find average prices have increased in Edmonton. The following is the average price of homes sold in specific years.

1969 - $21,050

1979 - $79,255

1989 - $89,099

1999 - $118,765

2009 - $326,049

2019 - $341,126

As you can see, there was a big increase between 1999 and 2009, and this was due to the economic boom of the early 2000s. Other than that, we have seen steady growth ever since. The price of land does go up. These numbers are approximate but could differ 5% each way depending on who you talk to.

TIP #22

'Be prepared to pounce on a great deal'

Positioning yourself for success is always key in the real estate market. When starting the process, it's important to get out and start seeing homes. Whether your process takes you a few days, or a few months, it's essential to get out and see homes. Who knows, you might eventually decide to buy the first home you looked at (after seeing other homes too), or you might buy the 10th home, or the 15th.

For example, if you are prequalified for $500,000 and you only want to be in a specific area that has 6 homes for sale, then let's go see all 6 homes! One of these homes may, or may not, work for you. But part of the process is to see these homes! This way, the next home that comes up in that area, you will see it and be able to make a fair decision on it because you already know what's out there!

You might wait and see a few homes that come up in the market before realizing that one of the first 6 homes you saw is the one you will buy. There are a lot of different ways this process can go, but the bottom line is that you need to see your options so that you can make the right decision.

If you are looking for an investment property or a flip, being prepared to offer quickly on a property is incredibly important. If you are looking at purchasing a fixer-upper for $225,000 with the intention of putting $25,000 hard money into it and selling it for $310,000, then you need to be ready when those deals come up.

If a single-family home comes up for $225,000, you must be prepared to go and see it on the first day it comes to market. If it's a suitable property, you must be prepared to make an offer. Those super cheap deals don't last long. Having a quick reaction time could mean that you save yourself, or make yourself, a lot of money.

__TIP #23__

'Ask your friends about their experience'

I believe that it's always good to get into the minds of your friends and family that have been through the real estate process before you have. At the same time, I'm always here to answer all your questions. But it is helpful to your own situation that you take the advice from your peers, as well as the advice I give you, and help formulate your best strategy going forward.

Generally, salespeople don't like when other people get involved with the customer. As an example, if you brought someone along to look at the home you are buying. Some Realtors feel it's unnecessary interference. I disagree. I welcome if you want to bring someone along that you trust. They might think of questions that you weren't aware of asking.

This helps you to think through the process in a good mindset while you have 2 advantages. Firstly, you have your friends that are looking out for your best interests. Secondly, you have me, as I will be more than happy to provide you with answers to all questions and give you my 2 decades knowledge. We are all here to help you and we are on the same side.

Before meeting with me, I urge you to come with as many questions as possible, so that we can have a fruitful meeting and get the process started right. By taking advice from people around you, you will have many proper questions by the time you get to me.

As I have stated previously in this book, no question is a bad question! I want you to throw all questions and scenarios at me as I want you to have a good understanding of the process moving forward.

TIP #24

'Looking closely during showings'

It's easy to get caught up in all the excitement during showings. I get it, it's a special time. However, we need to always look closely at different areas of the home that could potentially become issues. Those of you that have worked with me, you know that I sometimes point things out as a matter of importance.

If I notice potential issues with the roofing, foundation, grading, electrical, plumbing, and heating systems, then I will point these items out. While you are enjoying yourself during the showing, I will be in the background looking to make sure we don't miss any valuable points of interest.

For example, we will look at the roof and see if the shingles are in good shape or not. Are they flat or are they curling? Is this an item that you should be aware of? Yes. But these are also things that will come up in the inspection. It might not be worth your time to nit-pick at every minor issue. Just enjoy the showing and leave the other details to me. Relax and take in the atmosphere of the property you are viewing because it could become your next home.

It's important to also be aware of all the parts of the property. Let's make sure to see the basement, see the garage, see the yard. It may be difficult during the wintertime to go out and see the yard, especially after a huge snowfall. At some parts of the year, you might be limited.

In modern times, with permission, buyers can take their own photos and videos so that they can come back to the certain points of the house that they are thinking about later. Especially in the post-COVID-19 world now, videos have become much more common.

TIP #25

'The importance of the second viewing'

Buying a home is a big decision. Unless you have already seen many houses and you are ready to make an offer on the spot, then I always suggest a second viewing. This is a good thing because it gives you a chance to go home and think it over. It's never wise to make a rushed decision.

By the time you get back for the second viewing, you will be able to look more closely as possibly some of the excitement may have worn off from the first showing. If you are still excited, however, then it's a good thing. But still, I always suggest taking your time through the second showing so that we can work through all your questions.

Life is too short to have headaches. The second showing provides you an opportunity to confirm all your questions about the home, so that there are less surprises later in the process. Trust me, everyone hates 'real estate surprises.' Even if you are 100% sure about the property in question, go a second time.

The first showing is to see if you like it. The second showing is confirming that you love it! I always tell people that this is likely going to be the single largest business transaction of their lives. This is not to be taken lightly.

The second viewing will help you confirm all sorts of items that you may have overlooked on the first showing. Items such as age of furnace, roof, electrical panel condition, foundation, hot water tank, all plumbing, doors, and windows are some items that you may want to take a closer look at.

Let's be realistic here. You aren't going back to 'tear apart' the house by just looking for faults. You are just going to make sure you get a good look at everything before you emotionally fall in love with the home.

TIP #26

'Understanding the changing market'

If you bought a condo 5 years ago and you feel you overpaid, based on today's market value, you still don't call it a mistake. The market changes all the time, and values fluctuate. If your condo was purchased at a price of $186,000 5 years ago and now you can only sell it for $175,000, then yes, it is a loss.

However, at the time of purchasing the condo, the market may have been busy. If you hold onto it for another 20 years, then your mortgage will pay down and you will be able to sell it and make some money. But what if you must sell it at a loss? Is this the end of the world? No. But here's how to guard against these situations.

Normally, I like to give my clients an idea of future values of the homes they purchase. I will say things like "This will be easier to sell in the future because it has a bonus room." Or, you might hear me saying something like "The condo fees will never go lower, only higher."

I will give you the straight opinion of what I feel will happen in the future. Nobody can predict the market exactly, but I can use my experience to give you a better idea of what to expect going forward. I will sell you any property you want. But at the same time, I will give you the truth about the obstacles or advantages of when you go to sell it in the future.

The market changes, and what consumers *want* also changes. Understanding the market and where its going is a key element in the real estate process. You don't want to end up in a situation where you are having a difficult time selling a property that you are trying to move on from.

Guard against these situations by buying at a good price and choosing a property that is easier to liquidate. You will thank your future self.

TIP #27

'Your first offer is often your best offer'

As a seller, as nice as your home might be, you need to face the reality that not everyone who comes to see your house is going to fall in love with it. Even if the market is hot, your first offer might just be your best offer. Let's take a closer look.

You are selling in a hot market, and you put your house for sale on a Friday night. Let's say you get 4 showings on Saturday and receive one offer. Are you going to wait until Sunday for another offer? Or will you deal with the offer that is currently on the table?

What is the most likely scenario? The Saturday people that offered, they are serious and likely will give you an offer that is so good that you won't need to wait until Sunday for other showings or offers. If buyers are serious in a hot market, they will come on the Saturday to view the house. A serious buyer in this case wouldn't wait until Sunday to view the house.

Also, chances are that the Saturday offer is the most likely to close, as they were in position to decide right away that they loved your house. They probably had been looking for a while and thus, they had seen enough houses to warrant a final decision this quick. They won't have second thoughts when they wake up the next morning. When I go and collect the deposit cheque on Monday morning, they will have it ready.

If you wait until Sunday to review offers on your house, however, chances are that you have upset the Saturday buyer(s). Now, they are in a negative frame of mind. If another offer comes on Sunday, you have created a bidding war, or have you? Depending on exactly how hot the market is, this might not go as well as you like.

What happens if the Saturday offer drops out and the Sunday people offer you a lower amount? Even worse, what if the Sunday people call back on Tuesday and say that they have changed their minds. They made an emotional decision but now they have 'buyer's remorse.' Always take the first offer seriously!

TIP #28

'Selling in a slow market anxiety'

As a seller, as nice as your home is, it's important to realize that it may not sell on the first day. Price is the biggest factor here. The home must be priced at a level that is equal to market value at the time of listing. I have stated many times before that the market keeps fluctuating and pricing keeps changing. I will continue to mention this throughout this book because it's the truth.

Just because the house down the street from you sold for $540,000 doesn't mean that your house will sell for $540,000. You might sell for less; you might sell for more. Every home is unique. On paper, your home might compare exactly to other homes. We are talking about same square footage, same year built, you both have garage and finished basements. Other aspects can be different, such as finishing and colours.

Even though everything lines up, it still won't mean that your home will sell for that exact price. Be that as it may, the pricing will be close, if the houses are comparable in interior and exterior condition. When I mention close, we are talking within a 3%-5% range, give or take.

It's not just the houses that are different, the buyers are different too. Just because a buyer paid $540,000 for your neighbour's house, doesn't mean another buyer will pay the same for yours. Every buyer has their own specific tastes.

Moreover, buyers will look to customize the home after purchase. Don't get hurt feelings because the buyer doesn't like your paint colour in your living room. It doesn't mean that your paint colour is ugly, it just means that someone else their own ideas of what they want to do with the home.

In the end, with the right price and the right condition of your home, it will sell. And you will have a SOLD sign on your front yard, just like on the cover of this book!

TIP #29

'Communication, Communication!'

Throughout your experience, all lines of communication need to remain open. It starts with you, having to ask as many questions as you like. Beyond that, it's up to me to put you in position to understand the process as clearly as possible. All your other hired professionals need to be clear as well.

When hiring the right people, trust that your lawyer, home inspector, insurance broker, and mortgage broker will give you clear lines of communication all the way through. You are the consumer, so it's only right that you have a clear path of communication from everyone that's involved in your transaction.

I always make sure to get your questions answered in a timely manner and to communicate all dialect coming from the parties involved (buyer and seller). If you are in the middle of a negotiation, then it's imperative that the exact terms are negotiated back and forth, and you are told everything!

For example, you have made an offer on a home that is listed for $450,000. Your offer was $430,000. When we hear back from the other side, I always make sure to communicate everything told to me, to pass on to you. So, if they came back with $440,000, then I will tell you. Seems simple, I know.

But there's always other details to worry about. Maybe the seller wants a different possession date? Higher deposit? Shorter condition period? There's also the matter of the chattels, the appliances. We must make sure that we look over the entire contract, that's on me.

I will communicate all details to you in the negotiation to better help you make the right decisions moving forward. We will leave nothing to chance and make sure all is clear before moving forward to sign the final offer!

TIP #30

'What time is the best time for initial meet?'

If you know me, you know I am always flexible with time. After all, this is my line of work. This is what I signed up for back on April 23, 2004, when I first started my real estate career. Evenings and weekends are the norm in the residential real estate industry. It was like that in 1980, 1990, 2000, 2010, 2020, and beyond. It hasn't changed.

When you call me, be sure that I am more than happy to meet on an evening or weekend. The residential market can be extremely fast paced, so it's important to always be on standby in case things start moving quickly. Who knows, maybe a house that you want to see came up on the market in the morning and you want to view it that night. Let's go view it!

You cannot expect the same from other professions though. Lawyers mostly work the typical Monday to Friday, 9am to 5pm. There are some lawyers that do meet outside of business hours, so they can be sourced out if you genuinely want to see one outside of business hours.

Home inspectors are usually quite flexible too. They are known for working similar hours as Realtors and do their inspections on evenings and weekends. The only limitation they have is darkness. They prefer not to do inspections after sundown because it might take away from the inspection and they can't get a clear view of some exterior items, such as the roof.

Mortgage brokers are also generally quite flexible. These days, however, you might not even get to the point of meeting your mortgage broker in person. In fact, this will become more common in the future as the industry evolves. Many of them do take calls at all times of the day, so their flexibility is good.

At the end of the day, you are the boss. We all work on your timeline, so we must work around your schedule.

TIP #31

'How much deposit is needed for offer?'

I will say this only one time, don't be cheap with the deposit! A higher deposit shows more seriousness in the offer. It is purchase price 'dependant' to a degree. If you're buying a property that is $250,000, then a $2500 deposit should be the lowest. If you're buying a $500,000 house, then a minimum of $5000 deposit should be put down.

There is no general rule as to how much deposit one should put on a home purchase. You can put as little or as much as you like. If you don't remove your conditions, then you will get the money back, so don't worry. The best way to go about it is quite simple, just factor in your deposit as a percentage of purchase price.

For every $100,000 worth of purchase price, you should be putting at least $1000 deposit. So yes, for a $1,000,000 purchase, it is a cool $10,000 that you should be putting down. If you were thinking of only putting $1000 down on a $1,000,000 purchase, the sellers will not take you seriously.

With this all being said, there are builders that require a minimum of 5% deposit on purchases of properties that are too be built. So be prepared when going to a home builder, because they will require 5% up front before they start building your house.

In any case, come prepared with your cheque book in hand. I understand that many people in the modern world don't carry cheque books, but you understand what I'm talking about. Be prepared to provide a deposit when asked. There are many real estate brokerages that accept electronic transfer deposits as well, so that could make things easier.

Does the deposit go toward your down payment? I get this question all the time. Yes, it does go toward your down payment. Again don't worry, everything is under control. You got this!

TIP #32

'Are condition delays common?'

We always want to make the transaction as smooth as possible, but sometimes there are factors that are beyond our control. Over the many years I've been doing this, I have seen delays come in all fashions. It's important to understand that, in the world of finance loans, banks are going to be extra careful when giving out a 6-figure loan to buy a home.

In every year since I started in this business, obtaining a mortgage has become increasingly more difficult. Even if you have all your documents prepared, the banks might still come back and ask you for additional documentation to help complete the file and approval. This is what can cause delays.

For example, its Monday, and you have until Friday to complete your financing condition. On Wednesday, the bank comes back to you and asks you to provide additional work information. They ask you to provide documentation showing the number of hours that your spouse works per week at their job (On a joint application).

Your spouse goes back to human resources to request an additional letter stating confirmation of full-time hours. But there is a problem. The main contact at human resources is out of office until the following Monday, and they are the only person that can you provide you this letter.

I have seen situations like this before, and I have seen companies make it work for their employees, by having another superior draft a letter. This is not always possible, however, in larger companies. Larger companies have a hierarchy of the chain of responsibilities. Therefore, in cases like this, you would have to wait until Monday for that letter

An extension of conditions must be signed at this point. Situations like this are known to happen from time to time. Don't worry, it's not the end of the world. Banks will always err on the side of caution, so delays over minor things are common. They just want to confirm all aspects of the application before approving, and you can't blame them.

TIP #33

'Being patient during negotiations'

Once you have chosen the home you want, it's time to make an offer! This is one of the most exciting aspects of real estate, making the offer. Sellers can respond at different times. Some of them respond the same day, and most respond within 48 hours. With 'foreclosures' and 'estate sales,' the response time could take a little longer.

'Foreclosures' are generally handled by the banks, their lawyers, and the court system. If you were to write an offer on a foreclosure on Saturday, the earliest you will get an answer would be on Monday. All have their own departments that deal with these matters. Some banks take longer than others to respond. You should hear back on most of them within 5 business days. Judicial sales are the only ones that take longer because you need to wait for a court date. These type of 'foreclosures' get handled through the courts due to extenuating circumstances (For example 2 sellers that aren't cooperative).

With estate sales, a lawyer is appointed to deal with the transaction and the family appoints an executor, somebody to sign the offer on behalf of the estate and family. The executor is not a lawyer and can be available on weekends. But in many cases, they do want to consult with the lawyer before accepting any offer. As we have talked about earlier in this book, most lawyers work weekdays 9am to 5pm. Again, if you write your offer on Saturday, then Monday would be the earliest response time, like in 'foreclosures.'

Please remember to be patient throughout the process and always take time to think through the negotiation. When you hear back from me on what the counteroffer is, I always suggest taking some time and think about it before responding. There is no need to rush. On top of that, getting back to the other side too quickly, this might negatively impact your negotiation position.

When you exercise patience, you will show that you have no desperation to buy or sell. If the other side senses any sort of desperation, they will use it to their advantage and negotiations will not go to your preference. If I tell you to be patient, there is a reason for that.

TIP #34

'Be in position to walk away if need be'

In the world of real estate, never let yourself get pushed around. Regardless if you are a seller or a buyer, it is essential to be in the position to walk away at any time if negotiations aren't going in the direction you are comfortable with. It's essential to always maintain yourself and see the big picture.

If you are in position where you need to sell, we can work through it. If you are selling to buy a different home, then let's go one step at a time. Sell the house first, and then we go and find you your next home. If you already have another home picked out, then great, but still, we need to sell your home first.

If you get into a situation where you are purchasing a house before yours is sold, then you will be putting yourself in a tight situation. These situations are not fun at all. Plus, you have left yourself open to accepting a lower price on your home because you are in a hurry to sell. Be patient, it will save you money.

When you are buying, keep in mind that there are always homes coming onto the market. There are always new homes being built. So, if you miss out on a property that you may have wanted, it's not the end of the world. Opportunities will come and go, that's real estate, that's life.

I have been involved in thousands of multiple offer situations over my career, both on the selling and buying sides. I have seen many different situations. For buyers, I always suggest putting your best offer, win or lose. This way, if you win the offer, then you are happy. If you lose the offer, you are not disappointed because you made your best shot.

If you feel a seller is driving up the price by waiting to present your offer, then just walk away. You don't have time to play these games. Another home will come.

TIP #35

'The importance of understanding value'

Before writing an offer on any home, my job is to help you understand value, through your own eyes. The best way to do that is to get out and see properties. I have mentioned earlier in this book, you might end up buying the first house you see, or you might end up buying something we see after seeing multiple homes.

You gain more knowledge with each home you view. On top of that, I will be constantly pointing out features that will help grow your knowledge as we go. I will also be answering questions on the spot, during showings, so that you have a clear picture of what to expect.

By the time you have found the home you want to purchase, you should be able to understand value after seeing everything within your price range. This is particularly important because you will now have first-hand knowledge and expectation of how much you should be paying. Seeing it through your own eyes means a lot.

If we were to see 5 houses in the same neighborhood, with all of them being priced between $480,000 to $500,000, then it's a good bet that we will know the value being somewhere close to that price range. We will still confirm values prior to making the offer.

I can also show you comparable homes that have sold in the same area. These will be good indicators of where you should start your offer pricing at. Low offers can be workable depending on the price of the home and how it's priced compared to actual market value. Is it underpriced? Is it overpriced?

Thanks to all the knowledge that we will be receiving throughout the entire experience, you will feel comfortable making an offer at a workable price. By this point, you will know where to start. I am more than happy to give my opinion, but you are the boss!

TIP #36

'How long should you spend at a viewing?'

Typically, viewings normally last anywhere between 15 minutes to 35 minutes. I always say that you should stay long enough to see everything you need to see. If you have some interest in the property, then we can schedule another appointment to view again a second time.

With all this, you should never feel rushed. Take the time you need to look at everything. If you need 35 minutes, then take the 35 minutes. If you only take 10 minutes, then that's fine too. Sometimes, you might walk into a house and know right away that it's not the house for you.

I've been on showings that have lasted as little as 5 minutes. Sometimes, we would walk in and right away I would be told that they are not interested. For example, a home that was heavily smoked in, is something that you can smell right away. It can be a real turnoff to non-smokers and people with breathing conditions such as Asthma.

On the other hand, I have walked into homes, and I have been told immediately that it is the house for them. Although we would stay longer than 5 minutes, their decision to purchase will have been made within the first 5 seconds. This happens when a specific home comes up that the buyer wants, like in a specific area or price range.

Overall, the entire showing process should be done at your own pace. Fast or slow doesn't matter. The only thing that matters is that you find the right home for yourself and your family. It can take days, weeks, or months from your initial meeting. It truly depends on the pace you set.

Things are different when you enter a show home, as they try and keep you there if a long time if possible. But that's a different type of showing. Always take the time to hear out the salesperson and see what they have to offer. Initial visits with builders are usually around 30 minutes. Like with regular showings, you will take a shorter time or longer time depending on how much you like their product.

TIP #37

'How many homes should I view per day?'

The title of this chapter is a question I often get, especially from first-time home buyers. The answer to this question truly depends on you, and the type of home you are looking for. Usually, I would say to view no more than 5 or 6 homes per day. Anything more than that can just make the process confusing.

If you want to see a total of 15 homes, then I would suggest spreading it out over 2 or 3 days. I will always show you every home you want to see, but I also want to make sure that you are getting the most out of the experience too. If you were to see 10 homes in one day, then by the time we get to the final homes, you might be tired, and focus will be lower.

I've had people that only want to view 2 homes per week. That's totally fine too. Stretching out the process is Ok, because it gives you time to digest and process the homes we have seen. Everything will be done to the pace you wish it to be. I will be on standby always to give my professional opinion.

There are times when we must go above and beyond, to see more homes in a shorter period. I once had a buyer that had only 2 weeks to move. Yes, only 2 weeks! So, within these 2 weeks, we had to find a home, put an offer, satisfy the conditions (subject to financing and inspection), and get the paperwork to the lawyers in time for them to process everything.

The solution was simple, I told the buyer to pick out every single house they wanted to see, and we were to go and see them over a span of 2 days. Even though the buyer was rushed, they still wanted to explore every option. They got back to me with a list of 27 homes! Now it was up to me to coordinate.

Over the next 2 days, we saw every single home. On top of that, we were in the middle of a heat wave, so it was scorching hot outside. Luckily, they found the perfect house that suited their family, and we were successful in helping them close on time. Situations like these are not common, but when they come, I will surely be prepared. Let's go and find you a home!

TIP #38

'Buying a property that has tenants'

If you are buying a revenue property, then it is quite common to purchase a home that has current tenants. This applies mostly to 4-plexes, triplexes, and side-by-side duplexes. A clear point to make now is to say that you don't want to inherit horrible tenants. Don't worry though, because this is something we would easily become aware of during the showing process.

Single family homes that have been rented, however, usually sell vacant. The seller has moved on from the tenants or the tenants are planning to move out soon. I have sold many fantastic properties that were previously rented, so there is no real worry there either. But I have also showed many rented properties that had tenants who didn't care too much about the condition of the property.

To make your life easier, if you were to buy a property that was previously a rental (if the tenants are still living there), then we would have to take a much closer look at the property to help you to your final decision. It's a known fact that tenants do not care for a property in the same way an owner does. This isn't to say that all tenants are bad. In fact, there are many fantastic tenants that I have come across during my career. But it makes sense, an owner would care more than the tenant.

We also need to give 24 hours notice to view tenant-occupied properties. There are times when tenants make it difficult to view a home, and sometimes these are the cases you may want to avoid. Still, you never know until you view the property, so it's best to go if we can.

I have encountered many different situations in my career and have viewed over 25,000 homes. I have been turned away at the door by a disgruntled tenant more than once. These situations are known to arise so it's always best to be prepared for them, which I am. For the homes that we need 24 hours notice, I will let you know ahead of time.

There is nothing wrong with buying a tenant-occupied property to move in to. On a last point, if you are purchasing in a nice area, generally those types of renters give utmost respect to the properties anyways, so that is positive as well.

TIP #39

'Do condo fees ever get lower?'

Condo fees never decrease. I have never seen it happen and if it has happened, it's a rare occurrence. When buying a condo, it's important to know the monthly condo fee of the property you are interested in. Taking it further, you need to explore where the condo fees are going and if there is going to be an imminent condo fee raise.

As one of the conditions you should have in the contract when buying a condo, 'SUBJECT TO REVIEW OF CONDO DOCUMENTS,' should be included. In these condo documents, you will read up on the status of the entire condo complex. It will tell you of any major upcoming costs that might be associated with the condo complex.

Simply put, if the upcoming costs are higher than what is available in the reserve fund, then an increase in condo fees will be certain. There is no exact protocol of how often condo fees increase in condo complexes. It's a good bet that you should expect an increase possibly once every 5 years.

There are several reasons why condo fees increase. Inflation is one of those reasons. The cost of doing business is always going up. The condo complex must pay for accountants, contractors, cleaning companies, and management companies, to name a few. All these professions have shown an increase in cost over the years.

Other reasons for increase of condo fees include poor management of the condo board and possible litigation against the condo board due to some sort of business disagreement. I saw one condo board that was being sued by a contractor for not paying the fee of the service they provided.

The condo board agreed to pay $100,000 to a contractor to fix all the balconies in the building. The condo board paid $50,000 up front, with the other $50,000 coming at completion of the work. Upon final inspection, the condo board found the work to be extremely poor and decided not to pay the contractor. They had to get a different contractor, at $100,000 again, to complete the work properly.

The first contractor sued for $50,000. No matter how you look at it, the first contractor still held the first $50,000. So, the owners were at $50,000 loss. Condo fees up.

TIP #40

'Can I bring my kids to showings?'

Before COVID-19, I always welcomed buyers to bring their families to showings. When COVID-19 restrictions started becoming prevalent, us Realtors had to limit the amount of people we brought o showings. This went against my beliefs and business model, but we had to follow the rules.

Once we got past the entire COVID-19 scare, then restrictions were relaxed again, and showings went back to normal. All for the better because your kids are going to live in the home with you, so it's only fair that they get to come and see the home!

Some sellers get concerned because they have some valuable items in their home, and they don't want anyone to break them. Kids get into everything. Let's face it, it's true. When they get caught up in the excitement of seeing a house that contains a lot of toys, then they can become rowdy. Fortunately, I have been lucky enough to never have been involved in a situation where items have been damaged, but I have heard stories from other Realtors.

Personally, if it were my house I was selling, I would just put any valuable items in a place where kids can't get to them. If other items in my house were to get damaged because of kids playing during showings, I wouldn't lose any sleep over it. But that's me. Some sellers can get upset.

I have always been fortunate enough to have clients that had very well-behaved children. As I have stated, I haven't been involved in a situation like this before. But even though all my clients have had well-behaved children, there is always a chance that something could happen. Accidents happen all the time.

If you do bring your kids and something happens to break, please don't worry too much about it. I have insurance to cover it. Bring the kids, they will enjoy themselves.

TIP #41

'Warranties in brand new homes'

One of the advantages of purchasing a brand-new home is the fact that you can get warranties. To keep this explanation simple, you generally would get a short term 1-to-2-year warranty from the builder (which covers deficiencies such as settlement cracking) and a 10-year structural warranty.

No home is perfect. When builders build your home, they offer warranties because they know that there will be minor deficiencies going forward. Most builders that I have dealt with in my career are fantastic in this area of the sale. They have a systemized follow-up procedure that they enact, and they follow through.

For example, one builder I dealt with had a system where they would follow up after 3 months, and then again after 12 months. They would offer you to make a list of the deficiencies that come up, and if they are items that are covered, they will send their contractors out to fix them.

For the structural warranties, there are government syndicates that are designed to protect the consumer, and they are costly to the builder. By law, you must provide a new home structural warranty. These warranties are managed by government and have nothing to do with the builder. On top of that, they can cost upwards of $10,000 or more. Yes, these aren't cheap.

Structural warranties are acted upon quite rarely. In my career, I have come across many great builders that build structurally sound homes, so the buyers were in good standing and happy. If you do act on the warranty, they will arrange to send someone to your home and inspect the issue. Upon conclusion of their investigation, they will let you know if it's a major problem or not.

Buying a new home is great. But remember, I have never seen a house fall over in my career. Whether you are buying new or resale, you are doing the right thing by investing in real estate.

TIP #42

'Accurate measurements of homes'

In recent years, we have come to adopt an RMS system of measuring homes. Residential Measurement Standards. Our real estate board, and most real estate boards around the world, want to assure consumers that the size of the homes being marketed are accurate.

Upon listing a home, us Realtors must provide an accurate measurement of the home, either measured by us or by a third party. I always feel it's important to have accurate measurements of homes because, as a consumer, you want to know the details of what you are buying.

Luckily, our real estate board is extremely strict on the measurements of homes. They introduced the Residential Measurement Standards, and they strictly enforce it. This is one of the many reasons that it's smart to use a Realtor to buy a home. When making a private home purchase, there is no regulatory body that the private seller must adhere to, to provide you accurate information.

If a Realtor provides you information that is not accurate, you can always go to the real estate board to take up your concerns. A lot of times, wrong information is given on an accidental basis. Most experienced Realtors know that there is no point to lying and creating headaches for everyone involved in the transaction.

After all my years in this business, I can take one quick look at a house and I can tell you, on the spot, my opinion on measurements and if they are inaccurate. If you were to measure your home yourself, you might get a different measurement then I get. Everyone will measure a little differently, so don't get worried if your measurements are different than the other party. You should be within 15 square feet of each other. If not, then we will go through it together and measure again.

TIP #43

'Understanding different value points'

Homes in different areas have differing values. A home in an older part of the city, where they sell for around $300,000, is different than a home in a newer part of the city, where they sell for around $500,000. So, if your friend got a discount of 5% on a $500,000 home, it doesn't mean they will get the same percentage drop in a $300,000 home.

A 5% drop on a $500,000 home puts the home at $475,000 ($25,000). A 5% drop on a $300,000 puts the home at $285,000 ($15,000). Chances are that the bigger home has more room to move on their price. The smaller home might not have as much room to move on their price.

Taking this one step further, it's unrealistic to think that the $300,000 home will come down by $25,000, as the bigger one did. We are comparing apples to oranges here. Every real estate transaction carries a life of its own. No two transactions are alike. If your friends had an experience that was beneficial to them, good. I will always do my best to see to it that you have a beneficial experience too. The benefits you get out of the transaction might be different than your peers, but I assure you it will be a positive experience.

Different areas have different values. This is just the way it is. Once you get your mortgage pre-approval, then you'll know exactly where to start. As we start looking at homes, you'll learn very quickly what to expect with different value points around the city.

In my career, I have seen values change all over the country. Buying a home in Edmonton is much different than buying a home in Toronto. Buying a home in Winnipeg is much different than buying a home in Vancouver. Values are different everywhere you go. The important information to know is what the values are doing in your home market.

TIP #44

'The first offer is usually the best offer'

When selling your home, it's important to know that the first offer is usually going to be your best offer. Don't decline an offer just because you feel that someone else is going to come and give you more money. It could happen (someone coming to offer you more), but usually only in a hot market.

If your home stays longer on the market, it will look less valuable to prospective buyers in the market. If you receive an offer in the first week on the market, then you should strongly consider it. At the very least, make a counteroffer. If the home stays on the market for a month, you are unlikely to see an offer as high as the one that came during the first week.

For homes that remain on the market for longer than 2 months, buyers start to ask questions. "Why has this house been listed for such a long time? Is there a problem?" Most of the time, the only thing wrong with the house is the price being too high.

If your home has been on the market for a long time, then it's time to drop the price. Price doesn't fix everything, but it helps. If you drop the price, and get an offer right away, this is likely the best offer you are going to get. Buyers react to price changes.

When you are listing or dropping the price, always be prepared for the resulting action that will come your way on your home. Buyers react quickly to a deal that wasn't there before. A new listing is a deal that wasn't there before. A new price is a deal that wasn't there before.

Buying residential real estate can be a very emotional time for buyers. One should never make a business decision based on emotion, but in residential real estate, it always happens. That's fine, this is the home you are planning to live in and raise your family in. Enjoy the smiles and tears as they come.

TIP #45

'Always negotiate price over terms'

After inspection, buyers usually come back with a list of issues they want addressed, either through decreasing the price, or getting the seller to fix something. This also happens during negotiations at the beginning as well. Sometimes, buyers will ask up front for seller to fix or build something.

For example, a home with a partially finished basement. A buyer may ask the seller to finish the basement before possession. This can pose a serious problem because it might not get finished to the quality of what the buyer wants. I've seen associates of mine go through situations like this and they can get messy.

The way this would work is simple. Buyer and seller will agree on a holdback amount, in this case let's say $10,000, until the work is complete. A walkthrough would be organised a few days before possession to confirm this work is completed. If the buyer is not happy with the work, this could hold up the deal.

If the deal still closes while still needing the work to get finished, then that $10,000 will be held up and chances are, that both buyer and seller will end up in court afterwards. This is not fun for anyone involved. Therefore, I always say to negotiate through price. The only time you can't, is when something needs to be fixed urgently, such as a water leak or electrical issue. Those issues need to be solved quickly.

If you go through your inspection and find items that need to be fixed, then you would ask for a price reduction. Sometimes sellers will grant a price reduction, sometimes they won't. Therefore, it's important to negotiate properly ahead of time and understand the potential issues that might come up in the inspection.

I don't ever recommend using the inspection as a further negotiating tool, but buyers are free to use it as they wish. A lot of times, seller s won't budge on small items anyway. It just leaves a bad taste if you ask for $1000 price reduction if a couple of light bulbs are burnt out. Either way, always use price to negotiate what you want if you can help it. Again, unless it's something urgent, use price.

TIP #46

'Home inspector credentials and experience'

I have been fortunate enough in my career to have come across some great home inspectors. These men and women work hard to find any issues within the home, and they do a great job explaining everything. For first-time home buyers, it's especially important to have a good inspector that communicates as well as they inspect.

Personally, I have always found the best inspectors to be the ones that have some sort of background in contracting or trades related to construction. Inspectors that have had experience in general contracting, plumbing, roofing, concrete work, insulation, framing, and electrical can all be greatly beneficial.

Inspectors with major tickets in trades are even more helpful. A journeyman carpenter can easily tell you if the woodwork within the home is up to par. A journeyman plumber can tell you if all the piping is in proper placement and they let you know if there's any risk of water leakage.

I once came across an inspector that was a master electrician. This was extremely beneficial for the buyers because this guy knew everything about homes, top to bottom. Beyond his expert knowledge, being a master electrician, he could easily tell if the electrical in the home was up to code. Believe me when I tell you this, I have seen many homes that aren't up to code electrically.

A lot of times, when people finish basements, they don't get permits, unless they plan on renting it out. Without a proper permit, you could face potential issues with insurance if your house ever burns down. Never say never.

Fortunately, the master electrician was able to point out all the drawbacks and items of importance with the electrical panel that he was looking at. He gave the buyers a noticeably clear picture of what the issues were and what needed to be addressed.

It pays to have an inspector that knows homes. They are worth their weight in gold. When interviewing them, don't hesitate to ask them about their experience in construction, homes, and any other experience they may have.

TIP #47

'What is the cost of finishing a basement?'

This is one of my most asked questions in my real estate career. The cost of finishing a basement varies, but I know you don't want to hear a general answer. Let's break it down to numbers. These are not set numbers, only ballpark figures.

1000 square foot bungalow	*-$20,000 to $30,000*
1800 square foot 2-storey	*-$40,000 to $55,000*
2000 square foot bungalow	*-$50,000 to $70,000*
2500 square foot 2-storey	*-$60,000 to $80,000*
2700 square foot bi-level	*-$75,000 to $100,000*
3500 square foot 2-storey	*-$80,000 to $100,000*

As you can see, the price goes up as square footage goes up. Another factor to consider is regarding the quality of the finishing you are looking for. If you are looking for just a basic finish, then the costs would be lower. However, there is a problem with finishing for cost, I'll explain.

It makes no sense to finish the basement nicer than the upper floors. I have seen this with older homes. I have seen basements finished to a much higher extended quality than the main and upper floors. This is because the basement was finished in one shot, without the homeowner making any changes upstairs. Please, try to match your finishing, it does help your value.

The basement finishing should be at par, or less than the finishing upstairs. I'm not saying you must match everything, just be more conscious of what you are putting into the basement. The countertops, cabinets, kitchens, bathrooms, etc.

Most contractors charge anywhere from $30 to $50 per square foot for basic finishing. If you take your basement square footage and multiply it by $30 to $50 per square foot, you might get a number that is different than what I have proposed in this chapter. But please, keep in mind the fact that you need to factor in finishing to match or be consistent with the rest of the home. This will add or subtract from your cost.

Also, the type of finishing that you will put into a $750,000 home is going to be more costly that the finishing of a $300,000 home. Your finishing should match the price range of your home.

TIP #48

'Costs associated with buying brand new'

Whether you are buying brand new or buying resale, you are making your decision based on your needs and wants. There are always other costs associated with making your purchase, and we will get into them later in this book. But basic costs that come with buying brand new are as follows, landscaping and fencing.

Let's start with landscaping. In terms of cost, for a regular 5000 square foot lot, you are looking at a cost of anywhere between $3000 to $5000. A landscaping company can come and take care of the entire process, beginning to end. They will put the sod, topsoil, and grass. It also must be level where the grading is going away from the house. A good company will do it properly and it will get approved by the municipality.

For fencing, the costs can vary, but I will give you a good idea of it. Each side of your house should be a fence cost of around $3000. Usually people split that cost with their neighbours. So, your cost per side should be $1500 for each. Don't forget the back fence. Again, you should be able to split this with your back neighbors too. This makes it another $1500. In total, you are paying at least $4500. You could potentially pay around $9000 if you take on all the costs yourself.

In some years, the price of lumber is higher, so it can make this fence cost even more expensive. As an example, in 2021, the price of lumber nearly tripled for a period. With that increase in price of lumber, we had an increase in cost of fencing. Your cost could be potentially higher when lumber is expensive.

Usually, if you buy a home in a good area, you will likely have good neighbours that will be happy to share the cost with you. Just remember that your neighbours want that fence up just as much as you do. All you guys need to do is to hire a good company. Make sure to hire a good company! Don't hire cheap tradesmen. Just don't. Get reputable people in to do the job. They will do it right the first time and you will have no issues moving forward.

TIP #49

'Dealing with bad tenants in your property'

Zero tolerance. Don't put up with tenants that are going to give you headaches. It's easy for me to tell you not to put up with anything when I don't know the true full story. With that being said, I will make a few statements which will make sense.

If you have a long-term tenant that is going to be a little late on the rent, then you can be lenient. But ONLY if they have a good track record with you. By this, I mean that they have been a tenant of yours for at least 1 year and have not missed any payments. Also consider if they take good care of your property.

Beyond the tenants who have a proven track record, don't put up with headaches. I have seen many situations in my career where bad tenants have absolutely destroyed a property by the time, they have finished their lease. There are 2 main factors here, 1) Paying the rent on time consistently, and 2) Taking care of your property.

Termination of tenancy is required these 2 problems requirements are breached.

A client of mine asked me to serve tenancy termination paperwork to a tenant of theirs that hadn't paid rent for 3 months. I don't normally do this, but I was in that part of town, so I went. To my shock, I arrived at the same time as the 'Skip-the-Dish' delivery driver. Oh my God! These guys had no money to pay the rent but still were Ok to spoil themselves on expensive takeout food!

This brings me to another point. Blatant disrespect should not be tolerated. Some tenants will start to complain about issues that need to be fixed and start calling you a slum lord. At the same time, this is how they justify not paying the rent. They come up with excuse after excuse. Some of them might even take their issues to the tenancy board and file a complaint against you.

People like this are not worth dealing with. It pays to screen potential tenants carefully first. You won't have issues when you properly screen tenants. But the minute they do some sort of damage to your property, or are late on rent, don't hesitate to serve them with termination papers. No further comment.

TIP #50

'Can possessions happen on weekends?'

Possessions happen on weekdays, not weekends. The reason for this is simple. First, most lawyers only work business hours. Since the turn of the century, we see private contractors such as lawyers having more flexible schedules. But regular business hours will always be the norm.

Also, banks send the mortgage money to the buyer's lawyers during business hours. This will usually happen on the day of possession, or the day before. For possession, the money is sent from the buyer's lawyer to the seller's lawyer. And both lawyers must be working on day of possession. It will be hard to find 2 lawyers that are working on Sundays.

For brand new homes that are built, possessions generally happen between Tuesday to Thursday. Builders prefer mid-week possessions just in case there are any delays with lawyers or delays with something else with the home, such as contractor cleaning. They don't want to have to be dealing with some sort of delay on a Friday.

If a delay arises on a Friday, possession might be pushed to Monday. Builders and sellers don't want this to happen. A lot of things can be dealt with much easier during a weekday, compared to a weekend. The lawyers are readily available on weekdays, and not so much during weekends. Same with contractors. Sometimes, the builder might have some items they need to finish before a possession, and if the possession is slated for Friday, delays will happen.

You are more than welcome to arrange your moving for the weekends. But make sure to get all the business done and out of the way during the week so that you can comfortably move into your new home on the weekend.

All possessions that I have seen in my career have happened after 11am and before 4pm. The majority happen around noon. This doesn't mean that you must move in right that very moment. If you are at work, then I can meet you at the house after work. I will get the keys as soon as the lawyer says it's Ok. You can comfortably finish your work and meet me after, no problem.

TIP #51

'How do I handle multiple offers?'

There is no right way or wrong way to go about this. I have found myself in multiple offer situations over 1000 times in my career. I can safely say that each experience has been unique. There are a lot of moving parts when it comes to these situations.

The winning bid could end up below the list price, at the list price, or above list price. It depends on the buyers that are involved and their motivation. It also depends on the location of the property. If the home is in an exclusive area, then it will surely generate more interest, especially if it's priced low.

If you are a buyer competing in a multiple offer situation, then the general rule of thumb is the following:

1) Offer list price at the very least
2) For every offer you are competing against, offer an additional $5000
3) Understand that offers with less conditions will be considered more carefully by sellers
4) Put you best offer forward

For example, if a home is listed at $450,000 and there are 3 competing offers plus yours, then you would offer $465,000. You may or may not win the bid. This strategy will not always come out successful using this formula. But this is generally one way to go about this.

If you are competing against at least 2 offers, then you must offer list price at the lowest. If you are not prepared to go in at least list price, then don't bother with it. You will get out-bid. If a property is listed at a low price, then there is a high likelihood that it will sell above list price.

Upon writing an offer like this, I would do some research for you and confirm values. If the house is worth $500,000, and they have it listed at $450,000, then an offer of $465,000 is more than fair. Remember, every situation is unique. We will assess it on the spot and make the best decision moving forward.

TIP #52

'Confirming your bank pre-qualification'

I always tell buyers to make sure they have their finances in order before shopping for a home. It's not just a matter of your bank calling you and telling you they will give you a mortgage to buy a home. It's about sitting down with your bank or mortgage broker and knowing exactly what you can afford.

For them to give you a proper pre-qualification, they will ask you for your employment status. They will confirm that you have enough down payment to make the purchase. Lastly, they will check your credit. After doing these things, they will be able to tell you what your options are.

Never assume that you can get a mortgage easily. Even if you have stellar credit, a great job, and lots of money, you still need to get your affairs in order. I've seen people have trouble at the final approval phase because their bank or mortgage broker failed to adequately confirm all details of the application.

For example, I once had a buyer that had a quite common first and last name. In fact, there were over 1000 people across Canada that had his first and last name, spelt the same. Of those 1000 people, 4 of them shared the same birthday with him.

He was prequalified to buy a home up to $500,000. We found a home for a price of $475,000. We thought everything was going to run smoothly, and then things took a turn for the worse. A collection came up on his credit bureau. This was not his collection, there was a mix-up. His bank had pulled the wrong credit file, oops!

After a few days of cleaning up this mess, he was safely able to purchase the home. His bank did apologize for the mix-up, but it did still cause him a big headache. From then on, I always make sure to let people know to confirm things with their bank or mortgage broker. We don't want delays.

TIP #53

'Are virtual showings common?'

As the real estate world evolves, we are finding the use of cameras, videos, and facetime interactions much more common. Virtual showings are more widely used in commercial real estate, where someone from Toronto is looking to purchase a building in Edmonton. They will start out doing virtual showings through facetime, and once they narrow down their choices, they will fly out to Edmonton to view first-hand.

A lot of times, Realtors will do 'preview' showings of properties for out-of-town clients. As a Realtor, I don't mind doing this. But I will ask permission from the seller if I can virtually tour through the home or possibly do a short video. This is a common request, and it does help the process.

I will make a firm statement now. If you are buying a home that you will be living in, a virtual showing to start is Ok. But you still must view the property first-hand before making an offer! This should be an automatic thought in your brain. View the property in real life before moving forward!

Sometimes we will get sellers that don't want us doing virtual showings or taking videos. That's fine, they are well within their right to deny it. It is rare that a seller would deny this request. However, I have come across countless tenants that that have denied this request.

Their reasoning could be from several factors. Sometimes, they just want to be difficult because they don't want to have to move after the property is sold. Another problem they might have is with the condition of the property. They don't want that video to find the hands of the owner. The place might be in bad shape and they don't want evidence showing that they are not clean.

In the end, we will continue to see more virtual showings, especially in the post-COVID-19 world. But still, always follow it up with a showing in person. If you live and work inside the city you live in, then don't bother with virtual showings. Just call me and we'll go see the homes!

TIP #54

'How accurate are bank appraisals?'

Your bank will sometimes need to order a professional appraisal on the home you are buying. They do this so that to protect their interest in such case that you get foreclosed on in the future. The bank want to know that they can recoup their money should they take the property back from you.

These are generally a formality and while they are quite accurate, you shouldn't worry so much about the final value. If you get a great deal on a property, the bank will likely give you the lowest appraisal possible, anywhere from $1000 to $5000 above your purchase price. Appraisers aren't trying to make you feel good about your property value, they just want to show the bank that the value is there.

A Realtor can do the same job as an appraiser. The difference is that the appraiser has no direct responsibility to the client. A Realtor stands to make a commission upon selling a home, the appraiser gets paid regardless.

The use of appraisers is simple. They are a 3rd party that is hired to do a job. They owe nothing to the buyer and seller. Therefore, banks don't hire Realtors to appraise their homes. In fact, us Realtors can do the same job as appraisers. Appraisers have access to our sales data, and they use it to formulate their appraisal.

Appraisals are indeed somewhat accurate, but they are also very conservative. If you buy a home that is valued at $500,000, but your price is $450,000, then you have done well. If the bank appraises it at $460,000, again don't worry too much about it. A house is only worth what a buyer is willing to pay.

Pricing out homes isn't as easy as people think. There are a lot of variables when it comes to value. The market is always changing. The one variable we can't control is if there is a suitable buyer for your home, and how much they are willing to pay.

TIP #55

'Why is it so difficult to buy bare land?'

Banks give mortgages because they know you will be occupying the home. It is part of your monthly expenses. For bare land, this is an extra cost you will incur monthly, and banks don't like doing these unless you are putting big money down.

I get asked sometimes by buyers regarding purchasing their own piece of land and building the house they desire. It is completely doable, but you pretty much would need to buy the land with cash and have no loan against it. Therefore, it's easier to buy, because the amount of money you need to put down is much less.

To buy a land lot, you will need a minimum of 35% down. Even with this, you'd be lucky to get the loan. To buy a house, if you have good credit, you can get by with 5% down. That's a big difference. When you go to a builder, you're not buying the land. They have a program set up for you.

The builder will have access to the lots from the developer, and once you pick the lot you want, the builder will build the house for you. For many builders, this is a way of doing business. They basically buy or have access to that lot. It's just the same as buying a regular home. The only difference is that you'll have to wait 9 months for it to be built.

Unless you are planning to become a home builder, I suggest you be careful with the idea of buying a piece of land to build on it yourself. If you have deep pockets, then go ahead, but you may still encounter difficulties during the process. Banks won't make it easy for you. Without approved money, nothing gets done.

TIP #56

'Confirming down payment money'

I come across many situations where buyers are receiving their down payment from another family member, or they bring the down payment from out of country. For instance, Egypt or Lebanon. Banks need some sort of proof of where the money is coming from, because they want to guard against mortgage fraud.

I have had many clients over the years that have had their own money outside of the country. My advice is always simple. Once you start thinking of buying a home, start arranging to bring that money over. The longer you have that money in your bank here, the less headache you will have when trying to obtain a mortgage.

When you are receiving it from a family member, it must be from an immediate family member. You mother, your father, your brother, your sister, your son, and/or your daughter will qualify. They will have to sign a gift letter stating that they are giving you the money, not loaning it to you. Your cousin, uncle, or aunt will not qualify as an immediate family member.

In the end, if you want to avoid all these scenarios, then just get that money into your account as soon as possible and the bank will require it for 90 days showing. For the banks, once they see that you have had the money in your account for more than 3 months, then its clear that the money is yours.

It's always easiest when you have your own down payment. In the real world however, this is not always reality. In real estate, we must all work together to help you attain your dream of home ownership. I will say this one last time, if you have down payment money coming from family or out of country, start the arrangements to get that money into your account right away. Once you prove to the bank that the money is indeed yours, then we have cleared this hurdle.

TIP #57

'Please avoid smoking in your home'

In the 1980s and 1990s, most regions in North America banned smoking indoors. Before that, the smell of smoke was quite common at all facilities indoors, sporting events, malls, buildings, and houses. Although I wasn't old enough to practice real estate at that time, I can certainly understand how things may have been different.

With the ban of indoor smoking pretty much everywhere, the smell of smoke indoors is now very noticeable. Overall, many people don't like it. Even smokers, for the most part, will stay away from buying homes that are heavily smoked in. I personally know many smokers, and they choose to smoke outside, in their back yard or on their balconies.

Homes that have been heavily smoked in are less valuable than homes that have not been smoked in. Even worse, many people will walk into a heavily smoked-in home and then proceed to walk right out. This includes people with pre-existing health conditions or those with young children.

Once you buy your home, you are free to do whatever you like within the confines of your walls, apart from criminal activity. If you choose to smoke inside your home, just know that this will affect the future value of your home. This is no different than having other maintenance responsibilities, such as keeping your home clean and doing regular renovations.

After all, this home is your investment, and it is wise to do your best to protect this investment to the best of your ability. I'm not a doctor, nurse, or pharmacist, so I will not go into detail of the potential respiratory health issues that may arise from living in a heavily smoked-in house over time. I'm sure it's not the most ideal form of living.

A clean, fresh-smelling home is worth a lot. It's worth all the money you have put into it over the years and it's worth all the money you will put into it in the future. Also, make sure to clean your furnace at least once every 2 years and replace your furnace filter at least once every 3 months.

TIP #58

'Backing onto power lines and power stations'

There is a general myth out there that states it is unhealthy to live so close to power lines and power stations. I have heard people tell me that the radiation waves that come from these power stations, towers, and lines are harmful over a long period of time.

In my career, I have not come across any proven scientific study that proves this to be true 100%. It's unfortunate that people have these thoughts because it does affect value and saleability of homes that are close to these power items. I have seen countless beautiful homes go unsold because of their location relatively to the power items.

From a value standpoint, I can say that it does affect value and saleability. Sometimes, during showings, we would drive up to the house and the buyer would say 'no' even before going in. They would see the power grid behind the house, and it would be game over. On to the next house.

If you really looked closely, you'll see that these types of homes are generally listed at a lower price than other homes. Builders and Realtors alike are aware of the challenges that come with selling these types of homes. In the end, there is always a buyer for every home out there. Lowering the price will get it to sold.

I have walked into power-backing homes many times in my career. There have been homes that had an owner living there for over 30 years. The owners of these homes, the ones that I did meet, they didn't show no sign of health problems whatsoever. To keep it simple, they were alive. Backing onto power didn't kill them.

If you do buy a home that is awfully close to power items, then we need to make sure that you are getting a great price. The cheaper the better. This will give you more room to maneuver on price should you want to sell the home in the future. It's always better to be safe than sorry.

TIP #59

'What is a condo reserve fund?'

Every condo corporation has a reserve fund, or at least, they are supposed to have a reserve fund. Although its rare, sometimes condo corporations go bankrupt due to mismanagement of funds. Basically, the reserve fund is an allocation of money set aside by the condo board to cover future renovations needed at the complex.

The reserve fund is accumulated over a long period of time, and it comes from the collection of condo fees. Not all the condo fees go toward the reserve fund, just a small percentage does. The actual amount varies from one condo board to another.

For example, if you owned a condo and are paying $250 per month in condo fees, then the allocation could look something like the following:

$75	Utilities
$50	Maintenance
$20	Insurance
$60	Reserve Fund Contributions
$20	Management
$25	Security

Of course, this is just an example to help paint a picture of how it works. In this example, if your building has 100 units, then $6000 per month goes towards the reserve fund. Every year, you should be contributing $72000 toward the reserve fund. Knowing the reserve fund before buying the condo is essentially important.

When buying a condo, the sellers must provide you with the condo documents anyway. These documents provide all the information relating to the condo, they tell you how much money is in the reserve fund, and they show what expenses are forthcoming. This is vitally important, because, as we will see in the next chapter, this could become a costly experience if you don't look at these documents.

I've seen reserve funds as low as $50,000 and reserve funds as high as $1,000,000 plus. As a rule of thumb, there should be at least $5000 per unit in the reserve fund. A 100-unit building should have at least $500,000 in reserve if it is at least 10 years old. I say this because we need to account for continual expenses. If you had no expenses then the reserve fund could be higher, but this isn't a realistic expectation.

TIP #60

'Condo levies and assessments'

If you have ever owned an older condo property, I bet there's a good chance you paid a levy or assessment at some point. For those of you who don't know what these are, I'll explain in the simplest way possible.

Again, you own a unit in a condo building that has 100 units. The current reserve fund held by the condo corporation is $200,000. In the latest reserve fund study, it shows that the building is in dire need of replacing all windows. The quote comes in at $400,000. What happens now?

(A reserve fund study is a study completed once every 5 years on a condo complex and it gives insight into what needs to be done in terms of fixes and renovations. It talks about the existing lifespan of the current items, such as roofing, windows, doors, etc. It also gives a general estimate to how much these fixes will cost).

Since the reserve fund is only at $200,000, the other $200,000 will come out of the pockets of the unit owners. But it doesn't stop here. Condo boards need to always keep at least $50,000 in the reserve. And in this case, they might not want to use all the money that is accessible to them ($150,000).

The most likely scenario here is that the condo board will keep $100,000 in the reserve fund, they will use $100,000 from the reserve fund, and they will take $300,000 from the unit owners. Simple math will tell us that each unit owner must pay $3000 toward this, if levied. If you don't pay this, the condo corporation can foreclose on you, case closed.

In my career, I have seen over 50% of condo complexes (age 30 or older) have some sort of levy or assessment. You would think after 30 years that there should be millions of dollars in reserve. Unlikely. Over a 30-year period, condo boards turn over, people come and go. There is no consistency in leadership so therefore the money isn't effectively managed. It's important to be aware of scenarios like this before purchasing.

TIP #61

'Illegally renting your basement'

Before I get into this, I will state that there are thousands of illegal basement suites across the country that are being rented. I'd like to go on record and tell you that I don't recommend this at all. For insurance and safety purposes, you want to make sure that you are doing this properly.

If you were to do this, stick with just doing it using your own home. You live upstairs and your tenant lives downstairs. I guess this makes it more of a grey area, because you are just 'living in the same house' with the tenants. I would still form it into a legal suite before doing this.

If you were to rent it without having a legal suite, that person or persons down there would really have to be close and trustworthy to you. You would need to have access to the basement as well whenever you need it in case you need to fix the furnace or electrical panel.

A friend of mine once rented to someone he thought he could trust. They had a falling out and that renter reported my friend to the municipality. They reported that he was illegally renting his basement. If you can imagine, he had a real big headache out of this. The municipality sent an inspector to his home and forced him to decommission his basement stove.

Since we are on this topic, I will touch on the 'renting of rooms.' Young people that are single generally rent out rooms to their friends or people they know. The going rates that I have heard can range from $450 to $750. Again, if you are going to do this, make 100% sure you know these people well.

Overall, it is a great fact that, as a homeowner, you can rent out some part of your home and earn some extra income. This is one of the advantages of being a homeowner. Please, however, do it the right way and don't get yourself stuck in a situation that will only be stressful.

TIP #62

'Can people lose their deposits?'

I will go back to Tip #10 *'Avoid getting ripped off by shady people.'* The young husband and wife that had gone through an unfortunate experience prior to meeting me. They had tried to buy a house privately from a gentleman that asked for a deposit, and he put together the paperwork himself. They didn't consult anyone before signing.

As it turned out, they agreed to put a $2000 'non-refundable' deposit. First, these are rare to begin with. 'Non-refundable' deposits are only given with offers that have no conditions, usually because of a multiple offer situation. These buyers, however, were a young couple starting out and $2000 was a lot of money to them.

They never got approved for the mortgage. They went back to the seller and asked for the deposit to be returned to them. They were shocked to learn that the seller would not be giving that money back to them! Even when they were telling me this story, I could feel the heartbreak in their tone of voices.

In the end, they blamed themselves. They never consulted a Realtor before signing the contract. They put their trust in the seller and they got pretty much scammed out of their money. This was an expensive lesson to learn.

In real estate, you should never have to face a situation where you are losing your deposit. NEVER. I always make sure to manage the entire process carefully so that everything runs smoothly. Deposits are refundable before condition removal and the deposits are not held by the sellers. Our brokerages hold the deposits.

If you have a deal that falls through, then your deposit will come back to you in 5 business days or less. I am not in the business of losing your money. I am in the business of protecting your money.

I brought this point up again to illustrate the extreme importance of getting the right professional advice before signing anything! To some of you that have used my services, I may have shared this story with you. When it comes to money, there's no playing around. You work hard for what you have, so keep your money safe!

TIP #63

'Do I need a pre-approval letter?'

There are some sellers that want to see a pre-approval letter from your bank, before considering your offer. This used to be quite common as a practice a long time ago. However, I have only come across this scenario less than 5% of the time. On top of this, it is mostly prevalent with commercial real estate, not residential.

If a seller has gone through pending deals that have fallen apart over financing, then you can't blame them for wanting to see a pre-approval letter. Whenever the market gets hot, deals seem to fall apart more frequently. Buyers get all full of excitement with short windows of time to make offers. They end up changing their minds a few days later. Or worse yet, their bank says no because they have gone above their budget.

Banks and mortgage brokers generally don't provide pre-approval letters anymore. You are more than welcome to ask them for one and they are more than happy to provide it. In fact, having a pre-approval letter could help in the negotiating.

I have been involved in multiple offer situations where some buyers send in their pre-approval letter along with the offer. This tactic is used to show the seller that the buyer in on strong footing with their mortgage situation. When a seller is looking at 3 offers on the table for their home, looking at one that has a pre-approval letter will certainly help the case of the buyer.

It's important to mention that, even with a pre-approval letter, the price is what the seller will look most at when deciding. But any way you slice it, its good to use every tool at your disposal to help your bargaining position.

I once had a buyer that had made an offer of $775,000 on a 4-plex that was listed at nearly $900,000. The listing was overpriced, so the $775,000 offer was reasonable. The seller was considering accepting but they wanted to see a pre-approval letter. We called the mortgage broker and they provided one right away. The seller was satisfied and accepted the offer. Bargaining position my friends.

TIP #64

'What months are best for buying and selling?'

I have a specific way of describing how the market works in terms of how busy or how slow things are. In a seller's market, we are busy. In a buyer's market, we are slow. The following information is based on 90% of the time in a balanced market. This is also true for most markets in Canada 90% of the time, apart from Vancouver and Toronto.

JANUARY	-	BUYER'S MARKET
FEBRUARY	-	SELLER'S MARKET
MARCH	-	SELLER'S MARKET
APRIL	-	SELLER'S MARKET
MAY	-	SELLER'S MARKET
JUNE	-	BUYER'S MARKET
JULY	-	BUYER'S MARKET
AUGUST	-	BUYER'S MARKET
SEPTEMBER	-	SELLER'S MARKET
OCTOBER	-	SELLER'S MARKET
NOVEMBER	-	BUYER'S MARKET
DECEMBER	-	BUYER'S MARKET

Notice how I show an even split between buyer's market and seller's market here. 6 months and 6 months. Traditionally, the spring and fall months are the busier than the winter and middle months. If you are buying, then it is beneficial to buy in a buyer's market. If you are selling, then it is more beneficial if you are selling during a seller's market.

Overall, you can buy and/or sell whenever you want. I pinpoint these seasons of real estate to help show which times are best for you if you are intent on getting the best deal possible, buying, or selling.

Winter times are generally slower because people prefer not to move in the winter. Spring times are busy because families tend to prefer buying in March/April in order to time an end of June possession. The kids finish school, they can move comfortably, and then go on vacation in the first 2 weeks of summer.

The middle of summer is usually slower because people are away. Camping, going to the lake, and/or going abroad. You can choose to buy or sell any time you wish, I work year-round, and real estate never stops.

TIP #65

'Is it smart to make lowball offers?'

No, it's not. It's important to know that we need to be reasonable in all cases. If a house is listed at $500,000 and you want to offer $350,000, then I can assure you negotiations will break down even before they start. The seller, in this case, would reject the offer outright.

If a house is listed at $500,000, but the actual value is closer to $470,000, then an offer of $450,000 is reasonable. This would still be considered a low offer, but not a lowball offer. I will run comparable sales and see what the actual value is. Then we can determine where you should start with your first offer.

If you are still thinking of lowball offers, trust that sellers will not take you seriously should you decide to go this route. In the marketplace, sellers absolutely hate this. Sometimes, they get so mad that they decide not to deal with that buyer. If that buyer comes back with a more reasonable offer, the seller might still turn them away.

Real estate is a serious business. Having the expectation of buying homes over $100,000 under value is not realistic. I'm sure you may have watched TV shows about house flipping. A lot of those shows don't show the true essence of your marketplace.

I have seen people do house flips in this marketplace. Their profit margins aren't as high as you may think. They don't go around making lowball offers on houses. They simply find sellers that are willing to list cheap and sell cheap.

Talk to me before making this decision if you are seriously considering making lowball offers. I will give you every situation imaginable that might come up if you were to offer low on properties. I will give it straight to you and explain the pros and cons of lowball offers. Trust me, there are not very many pros, and there are a lot of cons.

TIP #66

'Proper etiquette during home viewings'

Respect of people's homes should be a given. I have been extremely fortunate throughout my career to have worked with people who show the utmost respect. Before COVID-19, I would always encourage buyers to bring along their children. Unfortunately, once COVID-19 came around, we had to restrict showings to a maximum of 2 people (usually to both spouses).

In the post-COVID-19 world, families coming to see houses has become normal again. With more people, however, comes more responsibility. Accidents happen, and things can get broken. Sellers don't usually leave expensive things out when they are selling their homes.

We rarely walk into homes that have expensive memorabilia, expensive vases, and things of that nature. If we do, I will always make a point to let you know so that we can make sure the kids are careful. Kids get excited, they can't help it.

I once accidentally broke a yard gate during a showing. Not purposely, I just didn't realize my own strength. Like I said, it happens. The gate was already a little faulty. I called the other Realtor and let them know. I have insurance for these things.

As stated, I have been fortunate to have dealt with some fantastic people in my career. So much so that I have never had to explain proper showing etiquette. Always respect the home you enter. There's only one last issue I will address here, whether to take off your shoes.

You should always take off your shoes unless the place is filthy. At that point, it becomes a question of safety. If we are viewing a 'hoarder house,' then we may not be safe to take off our shoes. If the place is filthy and the tenants insist on us taking off our shoes, then I would just suggest we leave. Nobody wants to step on a needle that has not been sanitized and used for bad purposes.

After COVID-19, there was a lot more emphasis put on not touching anything in the home. Therefore, some sellers request that children not come to showings. I don't like this but it's a reality we must face.

TIP #67

'Reviewing condominium documents'

When buying a condo, it's important to review condo documents prior to waiving conditions. A typical real estate contract has 2 main conditions:

Subject to financing

Subject to home inspection

For condos, you would add the following:

Subject to review of condo documents

The sellers provide the condo documents for your review. The only cases where condo documents are not provided are situations of foreclosure or where sellers are only offering the property 'as is, where is.' In any case, these documents always need to be reviewed, whether they are provided or if you must obtain them yourself.

The way to obtain them yourself is to go directly to the management company. They will provide them, at a fee. As the world evolves to become more internet friendly, condo documents can often be found online where you can order them direct. Before 2010, this was rare. But now, it has become quite common. The fees can range, for all the documents, from $200 up to $600. For high end condo complexes, it can be even more expensive. On condos less than $500,000, I've never seen a total cost be more that $550.

The are companies that review condo documents, for a fee. These fees can range anywhere from $300-$500. I personally believe that these companies are particularly useful, and they are designed to protect the consumer. It is well worth it, especially if you are a first-time home buyer. The following is some of the documents normally found in condo documents:

Reserve Fund Study

Financials

Information Statement (Summary of expenses)

Budget

Bylaws (For example if pets are restricted)

Meeting Minutes from Monthly Board Meetings

Meeting Minutes from Annual Board Meetings

TIP #68

'Don't miss payments in the middle of buying'

While in the process of buying a home, don't miss payments on anything! I have seen situations where pre-approvals have turned into declined mortgages due to recent missed payments on credit cards, car payments, and phone bills.

For example, I once had a buyer that received a pre-approval from their bank on April 1st. They had 3 months to start looking for a home, but they were in no rush. They called me at the beginning of May to start looking for a home that they would move into at the end of June.

We looked around and found a sweet little home that worked perfectly for them and their needs. It was under their pre-approval amount of $300,000. They were absolutely thrilled and delighted to finally become homeowners. However, not every story has a happy ending right away.

When they originally got their pre-approval, their credit score was well above 650. By the time we had made an offer on the home, we were well into the month of May. The lender, as part of their final approval, was just checking to make sure no major issues had arisen in the credit bureau. Unfortunately, there were problems.

The buyer had missed payments on all 3 of their critical payment set-ups, car, credit card and phone bill. Their credit score had gone from above 650 to below 550. Even though the responsibility was theirs, their lender also failed to mention to them the importance of staying on top of things during the approval process.

Another thing you don't want to do is go car shopping during this period. One trip to a car dealership could result in multiple hits on your credit. I once had a client do this, and between 3 dealerships, he got 13 hits on his credit! This is not a misprint.

Just please be careful and attentive during your approval period for a home. There is no sense in creating more headache.

TIP #69

'Viewing properties that are already pending'

Sometimes, in the heat of the moment and excitement, buyers want to view pending properties (Properties which already have an offer accepted and just waiting on conditions to be met). I don't recommend this. Earlier in my career I would show pending properties, but it doesn't make sense. It would be like approaching a person that is already engaged to be married and asking them to marry you. LOL, it doesn't make sense.

In organized real estate, over 80% of accepted pending deals are good and don't fall through. Less than 20% of real estate deals fall through. This doesn't give you much room for hope when looking at a property that is pending. Chances are slim that it will fall through, so don't bank on it.

If there is a property that you really like and want me to keep tabs on it while pending, of course! I have had situations in my career where a buyer client of mine has had the opportunity to bid on a property that was previously pending. These opportunities do come.

Overall, however, I wouldn't hold my breathe on it. While keeping tabs on the pending property, we should continue looking at options with other homes that come up. This way, you keep your total options open. Homes are always coming up for sale, be patient and the right one will come.

Sometimes, we receive a heads up if a property might come back to market. Beware, as these could just be tactics from sellers that don't respect your time. If I get a call telling me that a pending property is about to fall through, I will get complete confirmation before we act on it.

I once had a situation earlier in my career where we were told that a property was about to come back to market. The buyers got excited and wanted to write an offer immediately. The sellers then called back, after receiving our offer, only to tell us that their sale had been successful now.

Personally, I think this was a tactic using our offer to create urgency to make their current sale complete. So, confirmation needed because we don't want to be part of anyone's stupid and silly games.

TIP #70

'No room in real estate for playing games'

Even though we are in a responsible industry that is regulated, there is no shortage of 'interesting' situations that come up. There is absolutely ZERO time for engaging in little games that people play, like the example illustrated in the previous chapter. Like it or not, there will be people in this world that have no respect for your time.

The most prime example I can think of is the real estate market and how it was in 2007. Throughout Canada, that market was hotter than ever. Not since the late 1970s was the market so hot. The market in 2015 and 2021 didn't even compare to 2007.

There were multiple offers on properties every day. I know that Vancouver and Toronto have seen this for decades, but Markets like Edmonton, Calgary, Saskatoon, Regina, and Winnipeg only see this once every few years. When I am talking about multiple offers, I mean we were seeing anywhere from 4 to 6 offers per property, and sometimes more.

As things were starting to slow down (The market crashed in 2008), there was a lot of suspicion regarding the number of offers that were on the table per house. As a Realtor, I would call a private seller to find out how many offers are on the property, and I would be given a specific number that may or may not have been true.

Personally, I never experienced this with any Realtors that I was dealing with, but it was happening a lot in private sale situations. The market was so hot that it wasn't out of the question as to how many offers there was. And it was changing from hour to hour. The number of offers coming in would constantly change.

Therefore, I don't recommend buying privately. As a Realtor, I am obligated to disclose if there are any offers on the home and confirm that they are for real. For private sales, you never know what's going on. No time for games, this is your money at stake!

TIP #71

'Can I make money flipping houses?'

If you want to get into this business, there are 2 main things I always tell people. You must have at least $100,000 cash and you must have the ability to do high quality renovations. Without these 2 main things, making money flipping houses will be impossible.

If you are buying a home for $250,000, with the intention of flipping if for $350,000, then I will explain where this money is going:

Down Payment (20% down)	*$50,000*
Renovations	*$30,000*
Commissions and lawyer fees	*$10,000*
Up to 6 months carrying costs	*$10,000*

Notice how I said you need a minimum of $100,000? The 20% down payment is necessary for you to avoid any mortgage insurance costs, which will eat into your profit. Renovation costs could be higher or lower, depending on your costs. I always say that your renovation costs should be no more than $10,000 for every $100,000 of purchase price, or 10%.

Commissions and lawyer fees vary. Commissions are always 100% negotiable and there are no set rates. You can be paying anywhere from 2% to 5% of the final sale price. Lawyer fees are standard and don't change much. You can find yourself paying anywhere from $1000 to $1500.

When it comes to the renovation portion of the flip, you better make sure that the work you do is of the highest quality. Buyers that buy 'flipped' houses are aware of how much you paid. They generally don't mind paying your price, but they want to be sure the value is there.

If the renovation work is lousy, then you will not make money. Buyers are not stupid. When you sell a flipped home, the buyers are expecting it to be close to flawless, just as in a new home. If you have bad contractors, don't hire them for this type of work. The work must be of highest quality, or you won't get the highest price.

TIP #72

'*A house on my street just sold!*'

If you are ever curious about a home that recently sold in your neighborhood, give me a call! I'm always happy to catch up, talk some real estate, and answer any of your questions. Its natural for homeowners to always be curious and see how they 'stack up' against the other homes close to them.

But just because a house in your area sold for $500,000, it doesn't mean that your house holds the exact same value. If your square footage and features are similar, then your price might be close, but not exact. Houses are built with different floorplans, and as such, hold differing values in the eyes of buyers.

If you are looking to sell, then we probably will use that sold house on your street as one of the comparable properties to assess your asking price. We will also look at other properties that have sold in your neighborhood. There might be a house 3 blocks down which shows as a closer comparable because it has remarkably similar square footage and features.

Let's be real. It's normal to get excited when a house on your block sells. I get excited when I see sold signs in my neighborhood. I always check the selling price and the features. I find it's good way to keep abreast of what's going on in the market close to my home.

If there are certain features that have proven to be popular with buyers, then I would look to improve my home in the same way. For example, a home on my street that sold, it had a beautifully landscaped back yard. Before I decided to sell, I brought in a landscaping company, and I improved the curb appeal of my house by making the front landscaping look gorgeous.

TIP #73

'Why is curb appeal so important?'

What is curb appeal? Curb appeal is the basic attractiveness of a home from the outside as you drive or walk up to it. Great curb appeal is vitally important because it's the first impression of the home.

If you were out looking at houses, and we were walking up to a house that had a filthy front yard, chances are that you will be turned off even before going in. I've witnessed buyers go through this and it does affect saleability of a home.

I was once showing a home downtown that was clean on the inside but dirty on the outside. As the buyer and I walked up to the fenced-in front yard, all we could see what dog defecation all over the yard. This was a bad first impression. However, the buyer still wanted to see the inside of the house, so we went in.

The house inside was quite nice. It was clean and surprisingly well-kept. The floorplan was open, and the basement was finished. The furnace and hot water tank were recently changed out. The house showed 9 out of 10 on the inside. The problem was, as you may have guessed, that the house showed 1 out of 10 on the outside.

The buyer had already made their decision prior to entering the house. I made sure to let the listing Realtor know of the feedback and hopefully they were able to clean up prior to any more showings. The first impression had left a bad taste, and my client was certainly not going back.

If you are looking to sell your house, make sure to take care of the outside just as much as you would take care of the inside. Regular grass-cutting, trimming of hedges, planting some flowers, and keep from hoarding junk. Buyers view the outside condition as a particularly important aspect of the home condition.

Some people want to enjoy their yards when they move in. It's difficult for them to picture their yard being so nice when their first impression of it looks like a war zone. It doesn't take much effort to freshen up the outside. Curb appeal can make or break the sale.

TIP #74

'Why is it so hard to finance acreages?'

Many 'city' people dream of having a property outside the city. They dream of owning an acreage that they can sneak away to during the weekends. Central Alberta is well known for its many camping grounds and lakes. Some parts of Central Alberta are so beautiful, its worth a drive through it in the summertime.

Banks tend to shy away from financing properties that are outside the city or outside the town you live in. A bank will easily finance a house in the city because it will likely be your primary home. People will pay the rent or mortgage for their primary home. An acreage or lake property will likely be your second home. Banks aren't as confident.

As a property owner with 2 mortgages, if you were to lose your job and could only afford to make one mortgage payment, which one would it be? Would you pay your primary house mortgage in the city? Or would you pay your secondary mortgage on the acreage or lake? Easy choice.

The only way around the bank difficulty is to put more money down. If you currently have a mortgage in the city in which you put 5% down, then getting that secondary mortgage would cost you at least 20% down. I've seen banks ask for 35% down in these scenarios as well.

If you don't own a home already, then you must prove to the bank that the acreage you are buying will be your primary residence. The further out from the city it is, the harder it will be. Banks are more inclined to approve your mortgage when you live in the municipality where you work. If you work on the rigs, then the banks will look at where you have been living currently. This is why they normally ask for your current addresses and time living there.

Getting a mortgage on a property outside the city is difficult, yet not impossible. Therefore, make sure to listen to your mortgage broker and take in all their advice. They will give you a plan and get you into the desired mortgage that you need, while I get you into the desired house of your dreams!

TIP #75

'Government regulation in real estate'

For as long as I've been in the business of real estate, I have seen constant changes to rules and regulations regarding our industry. The government of Canada is always involved, and they mainly make changes to mortgage rules. They do this to keep the market even. They don't want it getting too hot and they don't want it crashing. Balance is the key.

Whenever the market gets too hot, the government raises interest rates or changes the rules to make it more difficult to purchase a home. Whenever the market gets too slow, the government lowers interest rates or changes the rules to make it easier to purchase a home. This keeps the market balanced.

Ultimate Capitalism doesn't work. As highlighted by the World Economic Crash of 2008, having too much freedom can be disastrous in the long run. In the United States at that time (2008), everyone was obtaining mortgages. While they do have government regulation there, it wasn't enough.

When COVID-19 came about, we had a whole new set of rules we had to follow. Realtors were considered an essential service, that was fine. But we were given a whole new set of rules to follow with respect to how we showed homes. We were limited to 2 people maximum in the house, wear masks, wear gloves, and provide sanitizer when needed.

In a case such as this, government intervention is needed to help keep the public safe. Even though there are many people who think too much government intervention plain sucks, it is necessary at times. Trust me, I have been frustrated many times with quick rule changes, but it's part of the business.

Overall, this isn't a book about politics anyway. Government will always be here to regulate, whether we like it or not. We just need to do our best to work within the parameters given to us, and we will be successful in the end.

TIP #76

'The use of electronic signatures'

As the world keeps getting more technologically advanced, we will keep moving more towards online work. With the advent of the internet, and particularly 'Windows 95,' we knew the age of electronic signatures would eventually come. A lot of Realtors avoided it, including myself, but it has made the industry a lot simpler.

Gone are the days when I would have to drive across the city just to get one signature. I don't mind doing it, but the e-signatures make life easier. Sometimes, when negotiating a deal, we would miss an initial or 2 on the contract on a Sunday night. Due to us wanting to make sure the paperwork is perfect, more running around would be needed. Now, a few clicks on our smart phone will solve that extra work.

For me, I avoid doing e-signatures with first-time buyers in the beginning. Buying a home is no small task. I would rather sit with you and explain the entire offer prior to you signing it. The purchase contract for a residential home is quite long, so its important to take the time to go through it before signing.

As we go through the process, we can switch to using e-signature ONLY if you prefer that way. I genuinely want you to understand the entire process from top to bottom, and I don't mind taking the extra time to help you get on that level. It's the right thing to do.

For people that have been through a real estate transaction before, the e-signature method is a great way to go. By having that experience already, we can cut down a lot of the time and we can focus more on the task at hand, buying or selling.

For clients that work out of town, e-signatures are perfect. Back when I started, if I had a client that was working up north on the Oil Rigs, they would have to go to the main office to find a fax machine or scanner. With the e-signature, the client can now sign from the comfort of their room in camp, without being bothered to run around looking for a means to send back signed paperwork. I stay up to date on all technology so that I can help my clients as much as possible.

TIP #77

'Why would I need Power of Attorney?'

If there are 2 owners to a home, and one of the owners will be going away during the sale process, then those 2 people must see a lawyer to sign a 'Power of Attorney.' This document will allow one of the sellers to sell the property and sign all the documents for it while the other owner is abroad.

This is common with husband-wife scenarios or siblings that share a property. I once had a listing where the wife had to leave the country to tend to family business. Unfortunately, her father had passed away and she had to leave, for good reason.

Meanwhile, her husband and kids stayed here as they were preparing to put their home for sale. To stay on track with their summer plans, they had to tie up her affairs before she was to leave, because she didn't know how quickly she would be back.

They went to their lawyer and signed the 'Power of Attorney' so that they could sell the home without her having to be here. The cost varies. It could be anywhere from $150 to $350. We ended up selling the home while she was away, and everything worked out the way they wanted. There's always a way around situations.

Unless you have an extreme situation, as in the one highlighted in this chapter, then there's no need to bother getting a 'Power of Attorney' unless you truly need one for your purposes. It's always best to sell and collect the money evenly and fairly.

When you do 'Power of Attorney,' make sure the person you are giving it to is trustworthy. I have seen these dissolve quite dramatically when it pertained to business partnerships. Be sure to take in the proper advice before signing one. This is especially true if the people involved aren't blood family.

TIP #78

'I have a limited price range, now what?'

I once had a client that was prequalified for $300,000 and the only neighbourhood he wanted to buy in had an exceptionally low selection of homes in the price range needed for his family (Millwood's). He wanted to buy a single family detached home, and there were only 6 houses in his price range.

He called me and told me that he knew the exact house he liked, and he wanted to see it. I arranged to show the house to him and his wife. I asked him if he wanted to see the other 5 homes in his price range and he said no. This worried me a little, but I figured I would talk to him in person at the showing.

I met them at the house and showed it to them. He was dead set on buying the home, while his wife wasn't so convinced. I saw that this was my shot, and I took it. I had to beg his wife to let me show them the other 5 homes before they made a final decision. She agreed and told me to set up the showings on the other 5 homes.

I didn't want to show them just one house before they made a final decision. I wanted to give them options and show them everything that was within the parameters of their price range and tastes. It was the smart thing to do and luckily, they agreed.

Once we looked at the other 5 houses, one of them stood out head and shoulders above the rest! They ended up buying that one, not the original one the husband was eager to bid on. Can you imagine buying a home without exploring your options?

Even if you have a limited price range, you should still give yourself options if its possible. Expand your territory search and be open to seeing different types of properties that fall within your price range. You are making a 6-figure investment into buying a home, so give yourself the opportunity to make the best decision possible.

How do you make the best decision possible? You make the best decision by viewing homes within your price range so that you can see, through your own eyes, what value means in your market. I already know the market. My goal is to help you see the market through your eyes.

TIP #79

'A clean property for showings?'

If you are selling your house, be sure to clean it prior to viewings! I can't tell you how many times in my career that I have walked into filthy homes. I'm just being real about this. I have been inside over 25,000 homes in my time as a Realtor, and I can honestly say that I have seen it all.

Buyers get a negative view on a home if it's dirty. Walking through a living room that's full of toys and clutter is not ideal. Buyers start thinking, "I wonder what else is dirty that we can't see?" They start looking closely at other parts of the house, the windowsills, the toilets, and the closets to name a few. The buyer slowly begins to lose trust in the home and the negative view can turn into the buyer just saying, "I don't like it."

As a seller, you need to be aware that buyers will judge you and your home. They are prepared to make a big investment to buy your home, so they will scrutinize it as much as they want. Buying a home is a sensitive and emotional time for buyers, especially first-time home buyers.

Stacking everything into the garage isn't the best idea either. Some people tend to stack everything into the basement too. Also, not the best idea. With selling your home, less is more. Don't hesitate to get rid of things you don't need. On top of that, make sure to stack things off to the side in a nice and organized manner.

Nobody wants to walk into the garage or into the basement and not be able to get feel the space. This hinders your selling as well. The buyer should be able to easily access all parts of the property with ease and comfort.

I once walked into a property where the tenants were smoking crack cocaine. They had all their drug paraphernalia laid out on the coffee table in the living room. And as you may have guessed, the place was filthy. We didn't bother taking off our shoes because we didn't want to step on anything.

I left it up to the buyer and they still wanted to view the home. I decided to lead the way through the house and make sure we weren't stepping on anything. Do you still think real estate is an easy job?

TIP #80

'Am I always safe at showings?'

I always promise you safety at showings. ALWAYS! However, I have encountered a couple of situations where my own safety was in question. There are many different scenarios that arise when viewing properties and it's my job to make sure it goes smoothly.

Some tenants can be uncooperative. I have never encountered one that has been aggressive in any way, but I always make sure to go early to these tenant-occupied showings. I will knock on the door, (sometimes they are home) and I will talk to them.

For the most part, cool heads always prevail. I just want to make sure the tenants are not aggressive in any way. The house I mentioned in the previous chapter, with the 'crack-smokers,' I did go in first and had a chat with them before asking the buyer if they still wanted to view the property. It was safe and there was no threat of violence.

In 2004 (my first year), I was selling a home in a trailer park and doing an open house. I decided it would be a good idea to go door-to-door in the neighborhood and chat with some of the neighbours. Maybe I could pick up another buying or selling client.

The third place I went to, the owner's dog came out and bit me! I was wearing a brand-new pair of Jeans, and the dog sliced right through it. I was bleeding! The guy at the place didn't seem to care. In fact, he had a good laugh over it. I wanted to kick this guy's ass, but I left. We exchanged a few words and I left. He didn't even apologize.

In 2018, I was bitten again by another dog at a house showing in the MacTaggart area of Edmonton. This time, my buyer client was upset and came sprinting to the front door (The homeowner was standing at the front door when this happened). I had to hold my guy back from attacking the seller in my defence. It was a dramatic situation, but I appreciated my buyer's reaction and willing to stick up for me.

In both 'dog-biting' cases, I made a full recovery. Please stay safe out there.

TIP #81

'Is there a tax if I sell my home right after buying?'

Capital gains! This is a loaded term in the eyes of real estate investors worldwide. If the home is your primary residence, then you don't owe any taxes on it. There might be some exceptions to the rule in different jurisdictions throughout the country though, I'll explain.

The key here to have a good accountant that can explain things to you clearly. As an example, if you work from home, then you might be subject to some sort of tax at some point during the process. If this sale of your primary home is being used as your primary income, then you might be subject to some sort of tax as well at some point during the process.

Being in the position of gains, it's a good thing. This means that you've made money in real estate. It's a good problem to have. Some people say that you need to live in your home for at least 6 months so that you won't be subject to any tax. As stated, different jurisdictions hold different rules, talk to your accountant.

It's become quite common for people to sell their homes quickly after buying. If you drive through a neighborhood that is only a couple of years old, I guarantee that you'll see enough 'for sale' signs. The world has changed, and the quick selling of properties is upon us now, and forever.

A good friend of mine, his family buys and sells a new home every 2 years. They buy cheap, they live and sit on the property for 2 years, and then earn a profit when they sell it. Clearly, they do it for financial reasons. But at the same time, it gives them a chance to freshen up their lives and add some excitement to it.

Obviously, they are well past the 6-month timeline that is assumed by many people. They don't pay any extra taxes. If you do this properly and stay within the rules, you will save yourself a lot of money down the line in tax expenses.

TIP #82

'How long do families live in the same house?'

In 2006, I showed a home that was built in 1955. The sellers were the original owners! 51 years in the same house! They bought the house once they got married. They raised their children in that house, and now they were selling. This was truly a rare occurrence in my career.

People generally sell their homes once every 3 to 5 years. As the world has changed, we have found that families don't tend to stay in the same home for more than a few years. There are many reasons why. Divorce and change of career are 2 of the most prevalent reasons why people sell.

I once sold a home for a couple a mere 6 months after they purchased it together. They weren't married yet, but the title was in both their names. I was a bit shocked when they called me to come back and list the house, but I need to do my job. That is real life. Real life happens and fairy tales don't always exist.

I once had a guy buy a home in the month of December, in 2011. In February of 2012, he was transferred within his company from Edmonton to Toronto. I sold the home for him in March of 2012, and he moved away. These things happen and therefore the average time living in a household has become so small.

Of all the homes that I have sold in my career, I only have had 2 buyers that stayed in their home longer than 15 years. One of those buyers sold after 16 years in the same home. The other guy, a great guy, has told me many times, "Sam, I will die in this house."

This brings us to the next topic, dying in a house. Are there potential issues that arise from buying a home that someone died in? Every person has their own take on this subject. For sake of this point, I would like it to be known that I have never visited a haunted house, nor seen one, in my career.

TIP #83

'Has someone died in that house?'

In 2009, I showed a house that was in foreclosure. We didn't know the full story about the house before viewing but we were in for a surprise when we went inside. The main floor was in rough shape, but that was to be expected. The basement, however, was in shambles. There were bullet holes all around the walls in the basement. Yes, bullet holes!

We didn't stay too long in the house, so we never examined too closely. There was no blood, although I'm sure if there was, it was cleaned thoroughly. We weren't sure what to make of it, but it was a clear assumption that someone may have been killed inside the home. We didn't investigate further; the buyer was not interested.

In 2018, I showed an 'estate sale' home where the owner had committed suicide inside the home. The sellers were disclosing this information to anyone that was in position to make an offer on the home.

This isn't always disclosed because we never truly know what goes on behind closed doors.

We don't always know the history of homes. If you bought a '1955-built' home in 2020, there is 65 years of history inside that house that we know nothing about. There may have been a domestic disturbance call to the police in 1973, or the house may have flooded in 1987, we don't know. Sometimes, sellers have a decent knowledge of history regarding their homes, but most of the time, they don't.

With 'estate sales,' buyers are always asking me if the owner died of natural causes inside the home. It used to be a common occurrence a long time ago, older people dying in their homes. But nowadays, with technology and cell phones, elderly people are usually at the hospital by the time they pass on.

If you are worried about buying a home where something dramatic has occurred, such as a death, then just let it be known to me. It's Ok to have these types of concerns. Don't worry, it's not strange at all. I have seen it all.

TIP #84

'Should I purchase a rent-to-own?'

We see ads for 'rent-to-own' properties everywhere. Yard signs, directional signs, and online ads promoting this way of owning a home. I have nothing against this sort of real estate, I just don't deal with it. Whenever someone asks me my opinion of them, I always say READ THE FINE PRINT!

Firstly, if you can qualify for a mortgage, then you should just get your own mortgage to purchase a property. A 'rent-to-own' is designed for people that can't qualify for a mortgage immediately. To be clear, a 'rent-to-own' is a property that you rent with a first option to purchase. Normally, you pay a higher monthly rent, in which a portion of that money gets put away towards your down payment.

The length of these agreements can be any length of time, 2 years, 3 years, and up to 5 years. By the end of this term, you must buy the home. If you don't buy the house at this point, then the owner has the right to keep that extra money you put.

If you made a 3-year agreement to pay $1800 per month, of which $300 per month goes toward your down payment, then you will have accumulated $10,800. But if you don't buy the home, then the owner will keep that money and rent it to someone else or sell it to someone else. As I say, be careful!

I'm not going to sit here and bash 'rent-to-owns.' I think that they could work very well for people that need it. Read through the paperwork carefully before locking yourself in to anything. Realtors don't deal with 'rent-to-owns,' so you might be on your own when handling this sort of transaction.

Last point, the seller is taking on some risk as well. They are betting on the fact that you will buy their home at the end of the term, for an agreed-upon price up front. During this term, they are losing out on other potential buyers for the property. So, therefore they keep that additional money.

Over 80% of 'rent-to-own' buyers don't end up buying the property. It could be any number of reasons. Maybe they couldn't clean up their credit? Maybe they don't like the house anymore. Please look at all possible outcomes before doing anything on this front.

TIP #85

'Are last-minute approvals common?'

You have made an offer on a home on Friday June 4, 2021. You have given yourself until Friday June 18, 2021, at 9pm for conditions to be met. What happens if the approval comes in at 5pm on that Friday the 18th? What happens if the seller doesn't grant you anymore time? This is a difficult situation to be in. How do we navigate around it?

In real estate, delays are a part of life. Sometimes the banks take longer than we anticipate. Sellers can be accommodating to a point, until they have lost their patience. If we find ourselves in a situation where we are awaiting an approval that might be 'last-minute,' then then we must think ahead.

Within 3 days of that Friday June 18, we need to schedule an inspection tentatively for the Thursday or Friday. Some inspectors will not want to do this so we may just have to schedule one and be prepared to pay a cancellation fee. We should respect everyone's time. You don't want to be in a position on Friday where your approval comes in at 5pm and you have until 9pm to remove your conditions.

I have had situations such as this occur. We need to be on point with this as much as possible and guard against potential delays. It sucks being in a situation like this but sometimes when the market gets hot, these situations arise. I promise you that I will always be on top of these matters, but it's a team effort as well. If we keep all lines of communications clear, then things will work out accordingly.

People in higher price purchase brackets are Ok to do the inspection before the final approval comes in. They are Ok to risk the $500-$600 so that things won't be left last-minute. Personally, I am happy to do the extra work so that you don't have to risk that money. As I keep saying, I am here to protect your money!

Last-minute approvals do happen. I have had approvals come in a mere couple of hours before the deadline. If you get your bank all the documents they require, then you will not find yourself in this situation. But we never know, so that's why I am always prepared for all situations.

TIP #86

'Is it easy to buy a condemned property?'

If a property has been used for illegal purposes or it has damages so severe that it will affect the health of individuals living there, then the government (Capital Health Authority) will shut it down. The owner can rectify these concerns and take it back to government for inspection and approval.

A house that contains significant mold or exposed asbestos is a house likely to be deemed uninhabitable by the Capital Health Authority. Opportunities will be given to rectify these problems, but if the property is too old, then your only option is to tear it down.

From time to time, homes that are deemed 'uninhabitable' come onto the market. They are exceedingly difficult to finance as well. Banks don't like to touch these sorts of properties due to the high risk involved. You either must pay cash or go through a private lender that will undoubtedly charge you a high interest rate. But why would someone want to buy a property like this?

These properties, when they come onto the market, are generally very low-priced properties. Investors and flippers salivate at the prospect of turning these properties around and gaining a profit. These are people that have experience with properties of this sort. If you don't have any experience with these types of properties, then educate yourself first before stepping into one. I am always available for questions.

You bank will almost certainly say no unless you have a large down payment and can show a high income. Remember, banks only want to finance homes that you plan on living in. After that, when you buy additional properties for investment, you need to put at least 20% down.

In every year that I have been a full-time real estate professional, mortgages have gotten more difficult to approve. If you seriously are thinking of buying a condemned property, then give me a call. We can discus your options as well as all the pros and cons relating to it.

TIP #87

'Turn water of at vacant properties'

If you are selling a property that is vacant, make sure to turn the water off! The reason is simple, you may have a water leak and if you are not present, your next water bill could get quite steep. I once had a seller that this happened to.

They had a vacant townhouse that they had put up for rent. It had been a week since anyone had been to the property. It was the dead of winter, and the furnace broke down. The home became cold, and a couple of pipes had burst. His utility company had called him and told him that the water consumption at the townhouse was unusually high for 3 consecutive days.

He went over to the property, and he shockingly found that the water was spewing out of pipes in all areas of the house! He quickly ran downstairs and shut the main water line off. There was water damage everywhere, so this was going to be an expensive situation. The damages inside came out to nearly $10,000. But this wasn't the end of it.

The water bill came out to a whopping $4000! The homeowner was on the hook for the entire bill. This was indeed an unfortunate situation. Luckily, we were able to get around some of it. Prior to his home being vacated, I advised him to get the proper insurance in case of damage, flood, or fire for vacant properties. Insurance was able to cover much of the damages, thankfully.

The high-water bill, however, the owner was on the hook for. Even though he asked for a special circumstance waive of the fees, the fact remained that the water was used and had to be paid for. This was an awfully expensive lesson. If you know me, you know that I always ask that the water be shut down at vacant properties.

Unless you are willing to visit the property daily, then it's better to be safe than sorry with a situation such as this. Unnecessary expenditures are annoying and a complete waste of money and time.

TIP #88

'Is an 'open house' worth doing?'

'Open houses,' at the turn of the century were starting to become less common. With the advent of the internet and online ways of viewing homes (such as virtual tours), people would rather get the information from the comfort of their homes. This being said, 'open houses' are still being done.

When COVID-19 came around, many jurisdictions around the world put a temporary ban on 'open houses.' In Canada, we basically couldn't do 'open houses' for over a year. I love doing 'open houses' and I have done them frequently in my career. It gives a little extra exposure to the house and if the market is slow, it could help.

People rarely buy a home upon walking into an 'open house.' As soon as a home gets listed, all the information and pictures on it could be found online. In the old days, consumers didn't have this luxury. So, walking into an open house, and walking out with a contract, was normal back then. Before I got into the business, one of my brothers bought his first house upon walking in an 'open house.'

In the post-COVID-19 era, we have 'virtual open houses.' Realtors go live on Social Media during their timeframe at the house and answer questions. This is a cool concept, but the audience is limited to people on your Social Media. 'Open houses' should be geared towards people that live in the same neighborhood as the house in question.

If you genuinely want to get the most out of your 'open house,' then we must use my method. Whenever I schedule one, I go door-to-door in the neighborhood the day before, chatting with people in the area and asking if they have any friends or family looking to move into the neighborhood.

One spring day in 2016, I did an 'open house' that attracted over 30 people! The house was in a genuinely nice neighborhood, and it was overlooking a beautiful ravine. I spent a couple of hours in the neighborhood the night before, talking with people that lived close by, and it worked! We received an offer that night and sold the house! It pays to be aggressive. These results don't always happen so quickly, but we do our best.

TIP #89

'What is a homeowner association fee'

Some neighborhoods have a homeowner association fee (HOA fee). It can be anywhere from $150 per year up to nearly $1000 per year, depending on the expenses in your area. In Edmonton, I will use examples of 2 different areas.

Summerside is a neighborhood in Edmonton's south side. It has its own recreation centre and lake. Only people living in this area are allowed access to these facilities. Every homeowner in the area pays the yearly HOA fee and the money goes to maintaining this privilege for the residents. Summerside was well planned out and having the recreation/lake facilities have helped their home values.

Terwillegar Towne is another wonderful neighborhood in Edmonton that has HOA fees. In 2013, they opposed a potential low-income housing development that was to be built close to them. They had a lawyer on retainer, and they achieved their goal, to stop the potential development into their area. The people of this neighborhood were strongly opposed to this, and they made it known.

Neighborhoods that charge HOA fees are generally considered 'higher end' areas. These fees can cover all sorts of things. But the main things they cover are linked directly with the neighborhood affairs and how it affects the residents. Whether it's a recreation facility or hiring a lawyer to fight developments, HOA fees are designed to increase quality of living and/or protect the interests of the residents.

HOA fees are instituted by the developer at the beginning of the opening of an area. I have never seen an older neighborhood institute HOA fees. For an older neighborhood to do so, they would need all the residents on board, and that just won't happen. So, if you live in an older neighborhood, don't worry about these potential fees, it won't happen.

TIP #90

'Long-term maintenance of my home'

Your home is an investment, so you need to take good care of it for the time that you will be owning it. At time of purchase, a good home inspector will provide you with some sort of maintenance checklist for your home. I've seen many of these and I can say that they are extremely helpful and beneficial. They contain some of the following points.

1. *Change furnace filter every 3 months*
2. *Check sump pump every springtime*
3. *Clean out gutters every fall time*
4. *Maintain window wells around the house*
5. *Test smoke alarms regularly*
6. *Test carbon monoxide detectors regularly*
7. *Clean furnace every 2 years*

There are many more items that would be included in a checklist. I've seen lists as long as 100 items to check on a yearly basis. It's Ok, you don't have to go through the list 12 times per year or anything like that. But it's a great base to start from every year when looking at managing your upkeep.

When you buy your first home, you are taking on a greater responsibility compared to renting. When renting, if something is broken, you just call the landlord or property manager to get it fixed. If you own the home, then it's all on you. If you aren't handy, then I suggest you make connections with people that are.

When I bought my very first house, I got to know a handyman that lived on my street. Every time something came up that needed fixing, which wasn't often, I would just call him if the job were beyond my capabilities. It made my life a lot easier as well.

Make sure to keep all your warranty information if you are buying a new home or appliances. Or if you've gotten work done on your home, such as roofing or siding. Use companies that offer warranties!

Your home is your investment. Please remember that you will care for it more than anyone else would. When doing maintenance work, do it properly. Avoid taking shortcuts because it will cost you more in the long run.

TIP #91

'Do people still buy sight unseen?'

Buying 'sight unseen' means to buy a property without seeing it in person. This is a rare occurrence, but it still happens. There are foreclosures that come up from time to time where we don't have access to the property. If the house is mega cheap, then a buyer will take the plunge and make an offer without seeing the inside.

These days, with smart phones and technology, out-of-town buyers ask to see videos of homes prior to coming into the city to purchase. On the rare occasion again, some of them purchase without even seeing the property. They will go on what they see in the video and what their Realtor tells them about the neighborhood.

I don't recommend this at all. Avoid this situation. There are always more homes coming on the market. I realize that every situation is different, and your situation might lead you to make this type of purchase. I believe that people should physically view a property before buying it.

In commercial real estate, things work a little differently. Its not uncommon for a buyer to buy a building that they haven't viewed in person. In Edmonton, a lot of multi-family building owners are from Vancouver or Toronto. I have had buyers buy buildings without viewing them in-person. Usually, they would send a partner to view it for them.

It's all about the numbers. Buyers buy buildings based on how much rent the building is pulling in monthly. They aren't planning on living in it, hence why they don't need to physically view it.

I once had a buyer offer on a property that was listed at $250,000, and the value was minimum $400,000. Nobody was allowed to view the inside of the property. It was being sold 'as-is.' My guy wasn't the only offer. There were 7 other offers! All 'sight unseen!' The home sold for $280,000.

Under certain circumstances, as you can see, anything can happen in real estate. I will bet money that the person who purchased that home at $280,000 was a seasoned investor. If you aren't a seasoned investor, don't bother going this route. Always play it safe, especially if you are new to this.

TIP #92

'Design trends keep on changing'

Designs and trends change every few years and it's important to keep up with modern looks to your home. The following list details the design trends that have been popular throughout the decades.

1950s - Hardwood flooring became exceedingly popular and to this day, I see many homes that have the original hardwood flooring still in place. Although we now see newer hardwood flooring a lot, the preferred colours have changed.

1960s - This decade was all about the yellow appliances. Yes, yellow. I personally haven't seen a yellow appliance since 1995, so I'm not sure if they still make them or not. It's a good bet, however, that this trend won't be making a comeback any time soon.

1970s - The green carpets were all the rage! Carpeting itself had a big push in this decade. I have seen homes with the original green carpets, and I don't find them ugly.

1980s -   Wallpaper! This decade was all about the wallpaper. It gave an opportunity for homeowners to create nice designs on their walls, apart from the traditional solid paint.

1990s -   If you were to walk into a home that was built in the early 1990s, you would probably see pink carpets! I've seen a few of these and I don't know why it went out of style.

2000s -   Oak cabinets and oak hardwood flooring. This decade saw a return to the 1950s-style hardwood flooring.

2010s -   Dark colours were the prominent. Dark flooring, dark countertops, dark cabinetry, and dark backsplash. This decade was all about the dark kitchen features mostly.

2020s -   This decade has shown us that people have gone back to loving lighter colours. Lighter colours in the kitchens and bathrooms. Off-coloured flooring has become popular as well. We are talking about grey-tone flooring, which has never been a trend before.

TIP #93

'Grass alternatives in landscaping'

If you were to walk through a neighborhood in 1965, you would see nothing but grass and trees. Grass and trees on front lawns and in back yards. Take a walk through a neighborhood in 2021, and you'll see a much different view. Homeowners, especially in newer areas, use rocks as a means of design so that their maintenance is much easier.

For example, Many homeowners in newer areas put down rocks on each side of their house, instead of grass. It cuts down on lawn maintenance, but there's also a safety concern with it too. Many people don't want to mow their lawn at an angle as it can be dangerous (usually there's a slope going away from the house on each side).

Other forms of alternatives that we see on lawns is mulch around trees and more flower beds. With the importance of curb appeal to homes, as we discussed in previous chapters, exterior design of homes has become almost as important as the interior design.

Artificial turf is seen on an exceedingly rare basis. On the rare occasion that you see it, it will be on an expensive home in a lavish neighborhood. I can count on one hand how many times I've seen artificial turf on a house that was less than $500,000. It might become more popular in the future. Turf looks supremely ugly if not maintained.

Grass will always be the most popular form of exterior feature of your home. This will not change! Trees too. Grass and trees give your neighborhood some natural habitat to live in. Apple trees have always been popular too. Natural vegetation always hold value, no matter what the current trends are. I have shown houses that have apple trees in full bloom in the summer.

There will always be more creative ways to add to your exterior home design. Don't ever be afraid to try modern. Whether its grass, rocks, mulch, or artificial turf. You are only adding to the curb appeal of your home when doing this.

TIP #94

'Full disclosure is particularly important'

If you are a seller, don't hide anything! Seriously it does no good to hide issues from the buyer of your home. If you are a seller and you plan on hiding problems in your home, then I will not deal with you. I am all about honest business and I have no time to deal with these sorts of things.

If you were to sell your home knowing of serious problems and not disclosing, then the buyer has the right to take you to court. Thankfully, I have always had great sellers that I've dealt with, so these situations haven't arisen in my career.

If you are a buyer, then I'll make sure that everything about the home you are buying is disclosed. EVERYTHING. If everything isn't disclosed, then we will find out in the inspection anyways.

In 2011, I had a buyer that was purchasing a home in Millwoods, and we had an offer pending on it. They got their mortgage approved so now it was time for the inspection. We were told that the house was in great shape, and it seemed to be in great shape upon looking at it. The naked eye sees what it wants, yet sometimes the naked eye doesn't see everything.

The inspector found that there was a water leak in the attic and that the ceiling below the attic had been spray-painted white (it was sprayed over the mold). The seller did not disclose this to us, and we were upset. I recommended the buyer not purchase this house and they walked away. 2 weeks later we found them a house that was much better, and it ended up passing inspection.

When I'm helping buyers, even if issues aren't disclosed to us, I'll make sure to find out if there are any. I've been inside countless homes in my career so I can safely say that I've seen it all (I will keep saying this). When buying, if you get any sniff that the seller is hiding something, don't hesitate to walk away. This is your money, protect it!

TIP #95

'Please don't go over your budget'

If you are pre-qualified to buy a home at $400,000, then you should buy a home at $400,000 or less. There is no point to go to $405,000 or $410,000. Understand what you can afford and stay within the boundaries provided to you by your bank. If you want a home that is valued at $500,000, then you won't get approved if your approval was less.

It's a natural tendency for people to want to go to their maximum budget in real estate. After all, you are buying a place that you will be calling home. You want the best of the best; you need the best of the best. But by maximizing your budget, you run the risk of becoming 'house poor.'

I once walked into a $550,000 dollar home that barely had any furniture in it! The owners were sleeping on the floor, and they didn't even have a kitchen table! This was a listed house that I was showing to a buyer. The sellers were selling it because they couldn't afford to keep it.

You might get caught up in the excitement of buying a home and you completely don't realize the pitfalls you might encounter financially down the road. The excitement of buying your first home will quickly be forgotten a couple months into the future when you can barely pay your utility bills.

If you can't afford to buy the home you genuinely want, then it may be in your best interest to wait. Put off your search until you have accumulated more down payment, gotten a better paying job, and increased your credit score. It makes no sense to push on something that's not possible, trying to buy a home outside your limit. Your bank will decline you anyway.

Once you've taken the time to put all your affairs in order, the time will be right to buy the home you genuinely want. Patience can really pay off, especially in the world of real estate. You will comfortably buy the home of your dreams and afford to keep it, life is good.

TIP #96

'Should I invest in Real estate seminars?'

In my mind, it's always good to expand your knowledge of real estate. There are always great books to read, and good seminars to attend. However, some seminars aren't worth anything and they are teaching you things that you can learn from me. The only difference is that they will charge you $100 to go to the seminar and then will try to sell you educational packages for hundreds, or even thousands, of dollars.

I'm not in the business of selling information. The information I teach you is free. I'm in the business of selling homes. There is no seminar out there than can teach you anything that you can't get from me. The seminars to watch out for the ones that tell you to approach things differently.

In the early 2000s, some trainers were giving courses on a 'double close' technique. They would push this technique and promise that you will become rich beyond your dreams if you institute this method. What is this technique exactly? I will give you an example that will illustrate it perfectly.

The investor (you) puts a low deposit on a house (maybe $500) and locks it up. The investor removes conditions, and the house is now 'sold' and awaiting possession. The investor makes sure to put a long possession date as well.

While waiting for the possession date, the investor seeks out other potential buyers to buy the home from him at an increased price and have it close on the same day. If the investor is purchasing at $300,000, then they will try and sell it for $330,000 as an example. So, the profit is $30,000.

If the investor fails to find a buyer, they will just walk away from the $500 deposit and find another home to try this same strategy. This is completely stupid and not worth anyone's time trying. Before checking out any seminars, please don't hesitate to ask my opinion. I can only promise to be honest with you.

TIP #97

'The importance of 100-amp electrical'

Your house must have at least 100-amp electrical for your insurance provider to provide insurance on your home. These days, pretty much every house is built with at least 100-amp electrical service. In the past, houses were built with 60-amp service for the most part. You can still find these houses located in areas that were built in the 1930s and 1940s. I even saw a 40-amp electrical breaker in a house close to the University of Alberta in 2005.

60 amps (or 40) is just not enough for homes these days. With all the electrical gadgets we use, TV's, computers, hair dryers, stoves, microwaves, etc. If you draw more than 60 amps, or come close to it, fuses will blow, or the breaker will trip. Is it also a safety hazard? You bet it is! You can ask any master electrician about the drawbacks of low-amp electrical, and they'll give you many reasons to stay away from it.

Insurance companies refrain from insuring these properties for the main reason of safety. I'm sure it's rare for a house to catch fire after a circuit blows up. But you never know what will happen and electrical fires can start at any time. They know that in society today, we have a lot of things that draw power and 60-amp electrical just won't cut it.

There are some insurance companies that will provide you with insurance for the first 30 days of ownership, until you are able to upgrade your house to 100-amp electrical. However, if you don't get this done within the allotted 30 days, then they will cut off your insurance until such time you do.

Why is this an important point? Because if your insurance gets cut off, that breaches the terms of your mortgage contract. Your lender then can foreclose on you! Lenders don't mess around with this sort of stuff. It's their money that's at risk and if the house burns down without insurance, they're on the hook. Make sure your home has 100-amp electrical service and it will save you a lot of potential headaches and grief.

TIP #98

'What happens if I get foreclosed on?'

I often get questions from clients regarding the foreclosure process and why it happens. A guy that makes $100,000 per year, pays all his bills on time, and has never seen financial stress in his life, doesn't understand what it's like to be on the other side. He will never utterly understand the feeling of major financial loss such as a house. But this is real life and things happen.

"How does this happen?" There are many reasons that can start the steps toward foreclosure. Job loss, divorce, developing a gambling habit, drugs, alcohol, and a simple sudden loss of life motivation. These are all examples of things that can happen to cause a shift in life like this. You can talk to any homeless person in the entire world, and they will give you a story that will break your heart.

"What happens to me if I get foreclosed on?" You bought a home 3 years ago and you owe $365,000 on the mortgage. The house is worth $400,000. The bank takes the house back from you and lists it at

$388,000. They end up selling for $375,000. Does this mean that you are off the hook, and they will give you that $10,000 extra? Absolutely not! The bank has expenses to pay, mainly lawyer fees and real estate commissions. The following is an example of costs to sell a home for $375,000.

Selling price	*$375,000*
Mortgage balance	*$365,000*
Lawyer fees	*$12,000*
Real estate fees	*$15,000*
Total loss	**$17,000**

The bank has eaten a loss here and they might come after you for it. They might take you to court or they might just garnish your wages. Your only way out is to file bankruptcy. Unless your situation is dire, then you don't want to do that.

It's best to avoid these situations altogether. If you see yourself getting into a major financial pinch, then sell the house before the bank takes it. It's always better to get ahead of the problems then to face them after the fact. Banks can be ruthless when coming back for their money. One simple call to me and I can provide you options to get ahead of any problems.

TIP #99

'I've got 99 problems, but my house isn't one'

Home ownership is truly a special privilege. After a long day of work, you can come home and relax. Nobody can bother you unless it's your spouse or children. There are so many advantages to homeownership, it would take an entire book to go through it all.

If you can pay your mortgage and your bills, nobody can kick you out, not even your bank. When renting, you might be safe when you're on a 1-year lease, but once that 1-year lease is over, you must leave if the owner doesn't want you there anymore.

Homeownership provides you a freedom in this world that you just can't get anywhere else. You are never completely free in public or at work. At home, you are completely free to do whatever you want, eat what you want, paint what you want, build what you want….

I remember the first time I ever bought a property. The sheer excitement was intense. (Remember I'm a Realtor so I get excited with real estate experiences LOL). I started picturing where I was going to put the TV and furniture. I started looking at different colour schemes for when I was going to paint and new flooring options. This entire experience was exciting from start to finish.

You could have 99 problems going on in your life outside of your home. But when you get home, open the door, and go inside, you can forget about everything for a moment and enjoy the fact that your home is your castle. Nobody will bother you now.

I know some people that need to move every year because their leases expire, and they don't have options to stay. Don't settle for this in life. If you are reading this book, then there's a good chance that you want to take that next step into homeownership, if you haven't already. It's not a difficult process to buy a home, and it never will be. The pros outweigh the cons dramatically.

Having a solid base home to live in for yourself and your family give a peace of mind that you won't have to upend everyone. A young family with 3 children that must move every year, that's stressful.

TIP #100

'Why 13th floors don't exist in real estate'

Have you ever entered a high rise building and, in the elevator, you don't see a button for the 13th floor? Today, 80 percent of elevator panels don't have the number 13. You won't find it on the panels, and you won't find it in the stairwells.

While the 14th floor is the 13th floor for obvious structural reasons, many people don't like the number 13. Business owners, builders and developers tend to omit the 13th floor from office buildings and apartment complexes. This is done because they may lose out on potential tenants or buyers who refuse to live or work on the 13th floor.

When high rise buildings first came about in the late 1800s, builders would only build up to 12 floors. Partly because of the need at that time was less in terms of population, and partly due to the superstitions surrounding the number 13. When the need for bigger buildings came, builders started to skip the 13th floor as a means of habit.

Are you one of the many people in this world who suffer from triskaidekaphobia? This is a severe fear of the number 13. Personally, I'm born on August 13, so I've never had a problem with this number. But for myself, if I were to build a high rise, would I put a 13th floor? Yes, I would.

The world of real estate keeps changing. Although there are people out there that will never like the number 13, eventually there will come a time where consumer worries will be focussed on different things. Consumer wants and needs are continually evolving.

I guess my real point here is to point out that there's no use worrying about the little things. If you don't want to live on the 13th floor, then don't. Will it affect future value if you buy a condo on the 13th floor? I doubt it. I have rarely come into buyers that have superstitions with numbers.

There are people that don't want the number 13 to be part of their house address. Again, this is another superstition that some people have. And again, this is something that I've rarely come across in the duration of my career in real estate.

TIP #101

'Did COVID-19 change the market?'

COVID-19 didn't necessarily change the market. However, it did speed up the evolution of the market and how things are done. The world of real estate was already heading in the direction it was going anyway.

The use of esignatures became much more prevalent during the pandemic. It was already being used widely already. But once the pandemic hit, we really had to avoid face-to-face contact so that we could help 'save the world.' Eventually, this will be used 100% on all documents, and the pandemic sped up the use of it.

Open houses became less frequent. As we have discussed in this book, open houses were banned for a period. But even before the pandemic, open houses were much less used than in the past. They will never fully go away but, however, the writing is on the wall for open houses to be a thing of the past. As we talked about, virtual open houses might become more common, but not as effective.

With regards to viewing properties, homeowners will be a lot more conscious of the people viewing. There will be more emphasis on not touching anything. It used to be that as a Realtor, we are told to turn off all the lights before leaving. And that is still true for vacant properties. But now, for occupied properties, we are told not to touch anything. We leave the lights on, and we leave.

In 2009, I was showing a condo downtown and I accidentally left one of the lights on. The seller called me personally to give me a piece of his mind and let me know that I had missed one of the light switches. In 2021, I accidentally turned off one of the lights in a house I was showing. The seller called me and gave me a piece of his mind because I 'touched' a light switch.

Yes, the world of real estate has changed. Mostly in the ways things are done. The world has become a lot more sensitive now and while it may be a little annoying to view a house that has all sorts of restrictions, we must respect the homes we enter.

SUMMARY

'This book celebrates all of us together'

I've written this book in celebration of all the years I've been doing this and my appreciation to you, my friends, family, and clients. I could have never made it in this industry without you, all of you. The journey for me has been the reward.

I look back at all the experiences we've shared together and the experiences we will continue to share in the future. You are every bit a part of this book as I am. You are part of the stories; you are part of the words. For this, I thank you.

Ethics is a major part of any business. If you want to have a long-term success in real estate, then be ethical. What goes around comes around. If you tend to burn bridges, then you can be sure that it will come back and haunt you sometime in the future. Conduct yourself responsibly.

Being involved with real estate for so long, I have always found it important to maintain solid relationships with others in my industry. As I became more heavily involved as a Realtor, I found that maintaining these relationships within the industry is critical as I continually came across the same faces throughout the year in my work. When investing, dealing with clients, home builders, mortgage brokers, lawyers, and all other related professionals, you will need to maintain your credibility. The best way to do it is to remain honest.

I have had countless memorable experiences in this career. I have been inside many homes, seen many things, and met many people. If you are one of the many great people, I have dealt with along this path, you know me as a guy who has many stories. I am always willing to share stories if it helps to educate you.

When I first started, us Realtors will still using pagers. The younger generation now will likely not know what a pager is. Text messaging was just starting to become popular when I was starting out, but pagers were still being used. This is one of many changes I've seen over the years.

In the beginning of my real estate career, I had a full head of hair. Those of you that have seen my picture on my monthly mail outs, the picture was taken in 2009. Real estate can be stressful, but I don't think it's the cause of my hair loss. For those of you on my mailing list, I will not change that picture! It's the last remaining link to my hair!

The entire process of real estate should be an enjoyable experience. Whether you are a buyer or seller, the experience should be one that you cherish. Everyone should have at least some knowledge of real estate. After all, you are in an ownership position. If you are not in an ownership position, then after reading this book, I hope you will be.